Corfu

and the other Ionian Islands

Jarrold Publishing

CONTENTS

Looking towards Dasiá from Kontókali

Introduction to the Ionian islands

The Ionian islands lie off the west coast of Greece between Albania and the Peloponnese. The islands are greener and more pleasant than most of their Aegean cousins; visitors are not confronted with a strange world of barrenness and aridity. Thanks to more abundant fresh water, the Ionian islands are richer and more fertile than many in the Aegean and this makes a first visit to Greece very much easier.

These islands are also closer to us culturally than is the rest of Greece. Throughout history the islands in the Aegean have served as intermediaries between Europe and Asia Minor, and still bear the stamp of both cultures. The Ionian islands, however, unite two vital regions in terms of Europe's intellectual history, the ancient land of Greece, and Italy, which throughout the centuries has been a continually fruitful cultural source.

The Ionian islands are thus mediators between a world which is quite familiar to us, which has marked the life of Europe even in our own millennium through its literature, art, music, philosophy and science, and a Greece which in the same millennium has completely disappeared from our view — a part of the far more alien world of the Orient. The island of Corfu was the only part of Greece over which the Islamic Turks never ruled, and the other Ionian islands, with the exception of Lefkás, were subject to the Sultan of Constantinople for a very much shorter period than was the rest of Greece.

The Ionian islands are therefore ideal for those who approach modern Greece with caution and who do not wish to be thrown into a completely alien world. But they are also worth a visit by 'connoisseurs' of Greece. They hold numerous keys to a better understanding of the cultural and the political life of modern Greece. Throughout the centuries when other parts of Greece were suffering at the hands of the Turks, these islands became a refuge for artists, merchants, craftsmen, architects and noblemen who adopted western ideas and combined them with their own traditional ways.

Moreover, the development of an influential middle class, modelled on Venice, was to have a decisive effect in later times upon the political development of the burgeoning Greek state.

The Ionian islands also attract both those who know Greece well and first-time visitors because as yet they have not been flooded with tourists and therefore remain comparatively unspoilt. Corfu, admittedly, is an exception for this island has been a favourite holiday destination since the last century. Kings and queens, including the Empress Elisabeth of Austria and the German Kaiser Wilhelm II, were enraptured by this verdant island and returned over and over again. Nowadays Corfu is one of the most important holiday centres in Greece. With the exception of Paxos, the tiny island caught up in the wake of Corfu, as it were, the other islands are still little more than blank spots on the tourist's map. Large hotel developments are just as rare as places where back-packers with sleeping bags can spend the night. Correspondingly, there are far fewer organised trips or facilities for sporting activities available. The southern Ionian islands are therefore ideal for those who do not want to be organised and are prepared to do without some of the usual holiday facilities. You can enjoy in these islands a part of Greece which has not, as yet, changed its lifestyle for the sake of commercialism.

An unchanging lifestyle

Essential details in brief

Greece: Area: 131,944 sq. km; 9.97 million inhabitants. Capital: Athens (pop. 886,000; including the suburbs 3.35 million). Almost 20% of the country's total surface area is made up of islands, over 200 of which are inhabited.

Ionian Islands: Total area: 2260 sq. km; 182,600 inhabitants. This group of islands forms one of the ten historic regions of Greece (which however are of no political significance today), and is divided into four departments *(Nomi),* each administered by a prefect: Corfu with Paxos and Antipaxos, Lefkás, Cefalonia with Ithaca, and Zákinthos.

Corfu *(Kérkira):* Measuring 585 sq. km, Corfu is the second largest of the Ionian islands. It has the greatest population with 97,000 inhabitants and is roughly 62 km long and 4–28 km wide. The capital is Corfu town (Kérkira: pop. 37,000) and the highest mountain at 906 m is the Pantokrator. Corfu is one of the most important tourist centres in Greece and is very well developed from that point of view. It is not suitable for those seeking a solitary holiday but it caters for a wide variety of interests.

Paxos *(Páxi):* Area: 40 sq. km; 2500 inhabitants. The main town is Gáios (pop. 400). The island is covered with olive groves and its highest point is only 248 m above sea-level. Paxos is firmly in the hands of British holiday-home leaseholders and their guests and at the height of the season is no longer a quiet unspoilt island.

Lefkás *(Lefkada, Leukas):* Area: 292 sq. km; 21,000 inhabitants. The island capital is Lefkás town (pop. 6500) and at 1141 m the Stavrótas is its highest mountain. The island lies close to the Akarnanian mainland from which it is separated at its narrowest point by a channel scarcely 50 m wide. Lefkás is nevertheless the quietest of the large Ionian islands and, next to those on Corfu, its villages and towns are the most charming.

Ithaca *(Itháki):* Area: 94 sq. km; 6000 inhabitants. Its capital is Ithaca town which is commonly known as Vathí (pop. 2500). At 796 m the Néritos is its highest point. Ithaca is reputed to have been the home of Odysseus. In 1979 a group of German drop-outs settled here and since that time the peaceful, relatively poor island has become a favourite spot for young people. It also, of course, attracts those on the trail of Homer's heroes.

Cefalonia *(Kefallinía):* With an area of 717 sq. km, this is the largest of the Ionian islands, and at 1628 m Mt Énos is their highest mountain. There are only 25,000 inhabitants and the capital is Argostóli (pop. 10,000). The island has excellent beaches, a varied landscape and good hotels, making it a real alternative to Corfu, which nevertheless is generally considered more attractive.

Zákinthos: Area: 401 sq. km; 31,000 inhabitants. Its capital is Zákinthos town (pop. 10,000) and at 756 m the Vrachiónas is its highest mountain. Zákinthos is most popular with Greek holidaymakers, not least because of its rich vegetation and varied scenery. In 1953 an earthquake struck the island, devastating many of the villages.

The remaining islands: In addition to the six main islands, several smaller inhabited islands belong to the Ionian group. To the north of Corfu are Erikoussa, Othoní, Díaplo and Mathráki, and to the south of Paxos lies Antipaxos. People also live on the islands of Skórpios, Meganísi, Kálamos and Kastós which lie between Lefkás and the mainland. These islands are rather difficult to reach and are not geared to tourism. Kýthira and Antikýthira are often considered to belong to the Ionian group.

The Ionian way of life

Just look around you and it will very quickly become evident that the Greek inhabitants of the Ionian islands make a living from agriculture, in particular from the cultivation of olives. The Venetians were responsible for this as Venice needed oil, and what could be more simple than to compel the Ionian islands, which lay fairly close to their shores, to produce and deliver oil? In 1565 a law was passed forcing the islanders to cultivate olive trees. Very little financial aid was given and export was only permitted to Venice where the price was established and, of course, kept down.

It takes several decades before the first fruit begins to appear on an olive tree and thus it is an investment for the future of the family, a gift to later generations which will survive by centuries those who planted it. The fruit is harvested every two years and between the months of November and May dark-coloured mats can be seen everywhere on the island of Corfu. These are placed on the grass to catch the fruit as the wind blows it from the trees. On the other islands the same procedure is sometimes followed, but quite often the olives are shaken from the trees using long sticks. This is because on the other islands cereals or vegetables are frequently planted beneath the olive trees and it is not practical to wait for the wind to do its work.

Approximately 4 kg of olives are required to produce 1 kg of oil. Oil obtained from the first pressing is the best of all; oil from the third and final pressing was once used for lighting but today is utilised in industry.

After the olive tree, the vine is the most important plant grown on the Ionian islands, both wine and currants being produced from the grapes. Fruit of all kinds, including oranges and lemons, is cultivated, and so are potatoes and other vegetables. The cereals produced are not sufficient for home consumption and a certain amount has to be imported from the mainland. Many fishing boats can be seen but fishing is not important to the economy. For one thing the boats in the fishing fleet are too old and too small, and for another the Ionian Sea is not well stocked with fish. As a result of 'dynamite fishing' during the past decades — and there are some who maintain that it still goes on — stocks have been even further depleted. Pigs, goats and sheep are raised on the land but the lamb you eat in a restaurant would in most cases have come from New Zealand. Greek sheep are bred for their wool rather than for their meat.

There are no industries worth mentioning on the Ionian islands. The few factories there process mainly wine, fruit and vegetables; they offer very little work to the local people, and what work there is is usually of a seasonal nature.

It is no wonder therefore that the islands have become noticeably depopulated over the last few decades. Whereas in 1961 the population was 212,573, in 1981 it had dropped to 182,651. Cefalonia has been the worst hit by this decrease and Corfu the least affected, with a slight increase in population recorded here in recent years. Tourism, however, is the main reason for this and not the presence of the only large factory in the Ionian islands, which processes sisal, flax and jute.

While the other islands play a relatively small part in Greek tourism as a whole, Corfu ranks among the three most important and is second only to Rhodes and Crete. There is accommodation in Corfu for over 20,000 tourists – so many that in 1983 the Greek government banned the building of any more large hotels on the island.

Unlike the young people on the other Ionian islands, those of Corfu no longer need to move to Athens or even to emigrate abroad as there are more jobs in Corfu than

The open-air life

there are local people to fill them. For that reason seasonal workers now drift in from the mainland. The only youngsters who leave the island nowadays are those who wish to further their studies, for there is no university on any of the islands.

An alternative to emigration for the Greeks has always been to seek work on board ship. The Greek merchant fleet is the second largest in the world. Many of the quality houses on the islands belong to seamen who, separated from their families, have spent decades sailing the oceans of the world.

If you have the chance to see inside a Greek house, you will be astonished by its bareness. This may indicate a lack of money, but in any case furnishings play a far less important role here than they do in the cooler climates. The Greeks spend much of the year out of doors and prefer to spend their money on food so that nobody ever goes hungry. Olive oil contributes to the fact that the population's calorie consumption per head is somewhat higher than in many other countries.

Signposts of History

About 750 B.C: Settlers from the Greek city-states colonise the Ionian islands and develop them into naval bases, strategically situated on the way to the western Mediterranean. Corfu comes under Corinthian rule.

664 B.C: In the first naval battle ever recorded in Greek history *Corcyra* (Corfu) breaks free from Corinth.

5th c. B.C: During the long struggle for ascendancy between Athens and Sparta, the Ionian islands, with the exception of *Leukas* (Lefkás), fight on the side of the Athenian democracy.

4th–3rd c. B.C: The islands fall under mainland rule from Sparta, Macedonia and Epirus.

229 B.C: The first Greek town to be ruled by the Romans is *Corcyra* (Corfu), on the island of the same name.

148 B.C: All the Ionian islands are annexed by the Romans to their province of Macedonia.

A.D. 395: When the Roman Empire is divided, the Ionian islands become part of the East Roman Empire and remain Byzantine until the year 1081.

13th–14th c. A.D: Following the sacking of Constantinople by Venice and the participants in the 4th Crusade, the Ionian islands are ruled by various European princes and feudal lords.

1386: Corfu becomes Venetian.

About 1500: The Venetians conquer the rest of the Ionian islands.

16th–17th c: While the whole of Greece is ruled by Turkey, the Ionian islands apart from Lefkás remain under Venetian sovereignty.

1716: Under General Graf von der Schulenburg, Corfu withstands the last large-scale attack by the Turks.

1797–1815: During the Napoleonic Wars, the French, Russians and British in turn rule over the islands.

1815: At the Congress of Vienna it is agreed that the Ionian islands should become an independent state under the protection of Great Britain.

1821–1829: The Greek War of Independence against the Turks is waged on the mainland and in the Aegean.

1830: Greece is declared an independent kingdom, but the Ionian islands still remain a British protectorate.

May 21st 1864: The Ionian islands are united with the Greek mother-country.

1941–1944: Corfu and the other Ionian islands are initially occupied by Italian troops and then by the Germans.

1953: A severe earthquake causes devastation mostly on Zákinthos but also on the other Ionian islands.

April 21st 1967: The Colonels under Papadopoulos seize power throughout Greece.

July 23rd 1974: The military junta returns power to the civilian population. Konstantin Karamanlis re-establishes democratic rule.

December 8th 1974: In a referendum, 69.2% of the Greek population vote for the abolition of the monarchy.

January 1st 1981: Greece becomes the tenth full member of the European Community.

1989: PASOK, the Pan-Hellenic Socialist Movement, which has been in power since 1981, is replaced by a provisional government of Conservatives and Communists. Elections in October give no one party a clear majority.

⚜ Phases of History

Early Greek settlers

Odysseus is the first hero from the Ionian islands of whom we hear. If the poet Homer is to be believed, Odysseus was the king of Ithaca at the time of the Trojan War, approximately 1200 B.C. The islands were, of course, inhabited very much earlier than that; the oldest discoveries date from before 50,000 B.C. and consequently belong to the Middle Stone Age. At the time of Odysseus, the southern Ionian islands were very much under Mycenaean influence. At that time however a race of people unknown to us lived on *Corcyra* (Corfu), who some researchers think were Homeric Phaeacians although others identify them as Phoenicians.

It is evident that Greek Dorians settled in the Ionian islands in the 12th and 11th centuries B.C. but very little is known about this period. Indeed, the next firm evidence we have dates from 734 B.C., when Chersikrates led a group of Corinthian settlers from the Peloponnese to Corfu. That this island thus irrevocably became part of the Greek world is reflected in the fact that, at the beginning of the 5th c. B.C., the Corfiots played their part in the war against the Persians. However, when they sent 50 warships to Salamis in 480 B.C. these did not arrive until the famous naval battle was over.

Roman occupation

Cicero and the Emperor Nero were the most famous visitors to Corfu during the Roman period. Following in the footsteps of various other rulers, including the Macedonians and the Spartans, the Romans under the command of the Consul Gnaius Fulvius, and with the assistance of a fleet of 200 ships, conquered Corfu in the year 229 B.C. Within the next forty years the remaining Ionian islands were also subjugated. The north of Corfu became a popular staging post in later years for Romans on their way from the Adriatic Sea to the Aegean. On the passage out they could recover from the crossing of the open sea, which was often exhausting, and on the return journey they could wait for the wind to be favourable and for the sea to be calm enough not to cause seasickness.

The coming of Christianity

Jason and Sosipatros were the saints who brought Christianity to Corfu; they are reputed to have been pupils of the apostle Paul. The new faith did not flourish, however, until after the Roman Empire was divided into eastern and western parts in the year A.D. 395, when the Ionian islands came under Byzantium. In subsequent years the islands were plundered and ravaged on several occasions by foreign tribes including the Vandals and the Avars.

In 1081 Robert Guiscard, a Norman prince from Sicily, became the first of a new generation of foreign conquerors. He died soon after in the year 1085 on the island of Cefalonia, but his successors did not allow the Ionian islands any peace. They did not withdraw from Corfu until 1185 and the more southerly islands remained under their rule until 1209, by which time they had become no more than vassals to the Sicilian house of Hohenstaufen.

Domination by Venice

In 1716 Count Johann Matthias von der Schulenburg, a Saxon mercenary, successfully defended Corfu against ten-fold Turkish superiority. The power which

Former British Residency in Gáios

the Venetian republic had maintained since 1386 over Corfu, and since about 100 years later over the remaining Ionian islands, with the exception of Lefkás, was secure. As a result Corfu remained the only Greek island never to be ruled by the Turks during the course of its history.

French, Russian and British occupation

When Napoleon Bonaparte conquered Venice in 1797 he brought to an end an epoch which had affected the character of the Ionian islands as no other had done. French garrisons were placed on the islands, only to be taken over by Russian troops just one year later. For a short time, between 1800 and 1807, the islands became independent for the first time under the protection of the Russian Tsar and the Turkish Sultan. The French returned following the Treaty of Tilsit in 1807 and the British followed soon after. During the time of the British Protectorate the foundations were laid for the modern road network which now exists on the islands.

Union with Greece

King Otto I of Greece, of the house of Wittelsbach, was responsible for the fact that the Ionian islands were not able to become part of the mother-country following the Greek victory over the Turks in their heroic War of Independence. He was put on the throne in 1832 by the great European powers because they wanted a weak ruler who would easily succumb to their influence. It was not until 1864 that the Ionian islands were reunited with Greece when the Danish Prince William George I was crowned the second king of the country. On May 21st of that year, the people of the Ionian islands were able to celebrate the union with their mother-country for which they had fought for seventy years.

Archaeological discoveries

To be honest there are very few. If you wish to spend your time concentrating on classical studies then the Ionian islands are not the ideal place. There are no excavation sites where you can become transfixed with admiration as at the Acropolis of Athens, Delphi, or Ephesus in Asia Minor. All that the archaeologists' spades have uncovered in the way of ancient buildings consists of the bases of a few walls, or their remains, which tell the layman virtually nothing. Single graves, caves or the remains of Roman villas are just as unimpressive, and furthermore they are very difficult to find. Because they are of little tourist interest they are rarely signposted or marked on a map.

Nevertheless, for those interested in archaeology the few ancient sites on the Ionian islands have quite a special charm of their own. Almost everywhere you go, even at the height of the season, you will probably be the only visitor. There are no fences or officious attendants anywhere to hinder your enthusiasm or your research. The ruins, which are few and far between, all lie in the most pleasant of surroundings.

Because of the islands' association with Homer and the 'Odyssey' the archaeological sites on Ithaca and Lefkás attract visitors, as experts have connected almost all of them at some time or other with the legendary Odysseus. But the most interesting islands from an archaeological point of view are without doubt Corfu and Cefalonia.

Corfu: In 1812 French pioneers discovered the remains of a large temple on Corfu, which a good hundred years later was proclaimed by the German archaeologist Wilhelm Dörpfeld to be the Temple of Artemis dating from the period around 590 B.C. Kaiser Wilhelm II, who spent every summer on the island, even took an active part in its excavation.

The most important find from the Temple of Artemis, the Gorgon Pediment (a monumental relief), is on display in the Archaeological Museum in Corfu. As the museum contains other items worth seeing you should not miss a visit there.

Quite close to the temple you can see the walls of an early Christian basilica dating from the 5th c.

Cefalonia: On this island the walls of the ancient city of Sámi are particularly attractive. In many places they still stand several metres high and drive their way through isolated countryside high above the modern harbour development of the same name. Quite revealing, as it is unusual to find any so well preserved, are the late Mycenaean tombs close to the town of Travliáta. A Roman mosaic has been preserved in Néa Skála in the south-east, and the finds from the island's Mycenaean necropolis in the Archaeological Museum at Argostóli are worth seeing .

Trips to the mainland can be arranged for those who wish to visit other ancient sites (see page 50).

Gods of Ancient Greece

Zeus (identified by the Romans as Jupiter) presided over the Court of the Gods which, according to ancient Greek legend, assembled on top of Mount Olympos feasting on nectar and ambrosia. In order to obtain his power, however, Zeus had overthrown *Kronos*, his father, and *Rheia*, his mother. That was a family tradition, for Kronos himself with the support of his mother *Gaia* had had his father *Ouranos (Uranus)* cruelly emasculated. Zeus was married to his own sister *Hera* but he was not a faithful husband. Together they produced *Ares* who was the god of war, *Hephaistos* who was responsible for fire, smiths and craftsmen, *Hebe* who was the personification of eternal youth, and *Eileithya* the goddess of birth; but Zeus spent the greater part of his time in the company of other beauties. As the supreme god, he was naturally all-powerful, but he was also the god of thunder and lightning. Traces of the Zeus legend may be found particularly in Dodóna (see page 50).

Zeus

Hades (Roman: Pluto) was one of the two brothers of Zeus. He was the god of the underworld about which, of course, very little is known by the living, and for that reason he appears very seldom in art and literature. His wife, *Persephone*, whom he carried off from above ground, is perhaps more familiar to us. The couple were particularly revered in the Oracle of the Underworld *(Nekyomanteion)* at the River Acheron on that part of the mainland which lies opposite Paxos.

Poseidon (Roman: Neptune) was the second brother of Zeus. He was the god of the sea and also the originator of violent earthquakes. His wrath was to blame for the helpless wanderings of Odysseus. The tourist will come across his symbols, the dolphin and the trident, in many places, old and new, on the Ionian islands.

Artemis (Roman: Diana), the illegitimate daughter of Zeus and *Leto*, was worshipped mainly as the goddess of fertility but she was also mistress over animals, goddess of hunting, and the protector of youth and virginity, which she herself retained until the twilight of the Greek gods. The remains of a temple dedicated to her may be seen close to the town of Corfu.

Apollo, the twin brother of Artemis,

Poseidon

presided over the Oracle of Delphi, and was god of light and of the arts. He was also responsible for healing until this duty was taken over by his son, *Asklepios*. He was the only Greek god whom the Romans did not later rename, and has traditionally been looked upon by scholars as particularly representative of the Greek ideal of manly beauty. In Ancient Greece Apollo was regarded as one of the most powerful of the gods, and the major sites at which he was venerated, such as Delos and Delphi, were thus also important centres politically. A small temple in his honour was discovered on Corfu in the grounds of the castle of Mon Repos (not open to the public); the Roman copy of a classical statue of Apollo may be seen in the Archaeological Museum in Corfu.

Apollo

Dionysus (Roman: Bacchus), often seen as standing in stark contrast to Apollo, was the offspring of an amorous escapade by Zeus with a king's daughter named *Semele*. He was not only the debauched god of wine, however, but also the god of the theatre, in whose honour the theatre was originally devised.

Other gods ranking among the most important figures on Olympos were:

Hermes (Roman: Mercury), the messenger of the gods; *Aphrodite* (Roman: Venus), the goddess of love; *Demeter* (Roman: Ceres), the earth goddess; *Athene* (Roman: Minerva), the warlike virgin goddess who was also protector of Athens; and *Hestia* (Roman: Vesta) the goddess of the hearth. In addition to these gods, the ancient Greeks worshipped mortal demigods, the most famous of whom was *Herakles* (Roman: Hercules).

Artemis

Dionysos

The Greek Orthodox Church

The sight of the long-haired, full-bearded priests in their flowing robes and often encountered in the streets of Greek towns and villages will stay in your memory. The wayside shrines, like miniature churches, will also attract your attention. The Greeks may often be seen crossing themselves, and the number of chapels and churches both in the country and in the towns is almost incalculable. The Greeks are a devout race and 97% of them are followers of the Greek Orthodox faith.

The Orthodox Church detached itself from the Roman Catholic Church in 1054, but the reason for the schism goes back further than that. The foundations were laid in the year 395 at the time of the division of the Roman Empire. It is called Orthodox because it retained in its liturgy the same unchanged rituals, hymns and prayers which the early Christians had developed. Orthodox Christians do not recognise the Pope as head of the Church nor do they accept the dogma of his infallibility. Therefore, although steps are being taken to bring the two Churches together within the ecumenical framework, these attempts face major obstacles.

Orthodox priests may be married but such marriages must have taken place prior to ordination, and married Greek priests must abandon all thoughts of promotion within the ecclesiastical hierarchy. Only single men are chosen as bishops and for that reason the majority of bishops in Greece have had a monastic background. Their income derives partly from a salary paid by the Church, which still owns over 120,000 hectares of land and in addition is financially supported by the State on an annual basis, and partly from the fees earned from baptisms, weddings and funerals.

The priest's most important ceremony is divine worship, the *Liturgia*. Participation

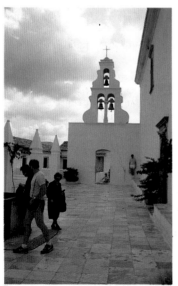

The monastery at Paleokastrítsa

in a service, if only for a few minutes in order to sense the unfamiliar atmosphere, is an experience no holidaymaker should miss. When you look around the church you will notice some essential differences from churches in the UK. Statues and other sculptures do not feature at all. Instead of these every church is decorated with *icons*, the sacred pictures always found in eastern churches. Icons are fundamentally different from our church paintings and are actually worshipped as sacred. Painters of icons are allowed no artistic freedom or any opportunity to be creative. The icon must always be produced strictly according to the canon which has remained unchanged for almost 1200 years. These icons also decorate the *iconostasis*, a screen between the body of the church and the sanctuary which the laity may not enter.

The most important festival of the Orthodox Church is not Christmas but Easter.

✄ Festivals and traditional events

Religious festivals

In Greece the major festivals are those in the Church calendar. Easter is the most important festival of the year and it is well worth visiting the country at that time.

Easter. Beginning in Holy Week church services are held twice daily, and as a sign of mourning the priests wear black robes. On Good Friday, national flags flutter at half-mast all day long, while many elderly people eat only lettuce leaves dipped in vinegar as a reminder that, on the point of death, Christ's lips were moistened with vinegar. People attend church several times on this day and processions take place in almost every village and town in the country.

Shortly before midnight on Easter Saturday, everybody congregates inside or in front of the churches. The people hold white, unlit candles in their hands and the interiors of the churches are in almost complete darkness. On the stroke of midnight the cry rings out, '*Christós anésti*' (Christ is risen); everywhere the candles are lit and fireworks illuminate the sky. From now on the greeting for the next two days is '*Christós anésti*', to which is given the reply '*Alithós anésti*' (Yes, indeed He is risen).

After midnight mass, the people gather at home or in a restaurant with the whole family and many friends. Eggs dyed red appear on the tables, followed by a thick soup made from lamb's offal, vegetables, onions, herbs and a lemon sauce bound together with egg *(mayerítsa)*. Everywhere on the morning of Easter Sunday whole lambs and goats turn on spits over open fires. They are eaten later at celebration meals and the day finally comes to an end well into the evening with wine, music and dancing.

If you wish to spend your holiday in Greece at Eastertide, you must plan well ahead as it rarely falls at the same time as it does in Great Britain. There is no hard and fast rule for calculating Easter. These are the dates for the next few years:

1990 — April 15th; 1991 — April 7th; 1992 — April 26th; 1993 — April 18th; 1994 — May 1st.

Christmas, unlike Easter, is hardly celebrated at all and Christmas Eve is without significance. Children do not receive their presents until New Year's Eve, which is otherwise spent predominantly in playing cards or other games of chance.

Carnival time begins seventy days prior to Easter Sunday and ends on the Monday before Lent (*Katharé deftéra*), when the whole family normally goes off for a picnic in the country. The forty-nine days of fasting which follow, however, do not tend to be much more strictly observed in Greece than elsewhere.

Panayíria, local church festivals, are quite significant. They are celebrated on the day which, in the Church calendar, is dedicated to the saint or biblical event commemorated in the name of the church. The size of the festival is determined firstly by the importance of the church, and then by the number of people in the community who celebrate their own Name Day at the same time. (This event is more important than a birthday in Greece.) Some panayíria therefore hardly attract the tourists' attention while others are true celebrations with the whole village becoming a place of festivity buried under a sea of flags and banners. The tourist offices on the individual islands will know exactly where a panayíri is being held.

The greatest of these festivals is the Assumption of the Virgin (in Greek 'Repose of the Virgin', *Kímesis tou Theotókou*), a national holiday throughout Greece, which is celebrated on August 15th.

Secular festivals

In addition to religious festivals there are, of course, secular ones. On March 25th the whole of the Hellenic population celebrates the rising of the Greeks against the Turks in the year 1821, which finally led to freedom. May 1st is Labour Day and on May 21st the Ionian islanders celebrate their union with Greece. On October 28th the population remembers that on that day in 1940 the Greek government rejected an Italian ultimatum and was thus drawn into the Second World War.

No festival without dancing

Whether it is a religious feast day or a secular holiday, when the Greeks celebrate there is nearly always dancing. Except in the discothèques, this almost certainly means folk dancing. There are numerous dances and the steps are usually extremely complicated with great demands made upon the artistic abilities of the dancers. As a tourist you should only join in when asked, otherwise it is more polite to stand back and watch. Only then can the Greeks fully display their dancing talents. The *sirtaki*, which is usually considered by visitors to be 'the' Greek dance, is performed mainly to please the tourists.

The Greek way of life

A few hours spent in a *kafeníon* are a good introduction to the Greek way of life. Take a seat and wait to see what happens. As a rule, nothing very much at first. The kafeníon is the place where the Greek spends a good deal of his time and it would be unwise to be constantly drinking. For that reason, the landlord or the waiter will not bother the customer until the latter wishes to order something, even if that takes as long as an hour. In the meantime the customer takes the opportunity to hear the most recent news from near and far and to discuss this and politics in general with his companions. Business can be negotiated and terms arrived at. Various games are played in the kafeníon: cards, draughts or the Greek national game *távli*, which is the equivalent of backgammon. Perhaps the customer, waiting patiently, has made an appointment to meet someone. Punctuality is not exactly a Greek virtue, except when it concerns bus, ship and air timetables.

The Greek often whiles away his time with the *komboloí*, a string of plastic, glass, amber or silver beads which looks very much like a rosary. It has, however,

No festival without dancing

no Christian religious significance whatsoever as the Greeks developed it from the Turkish rosary, which consisted of ninety-nine pearls representing the ninety-nine names of Allah. As it was difficult to play with that number of pearls, the Greek komboloia only have thirteen, fifteen or seventeen pieces. You can also get huge, quite bulky ones which are not played with but are used as wall decorations or lucky mascots. The name komboloí derives from the *kombos* (knot) which holds the string together at the top. The knot is a good-luck symbol for the Greeks. If one is tied in a handkerchief, it is not done as a reminder but for luck in tricky situations.

Time passes. The Greeks usually order themselves just a coffee but it is always accompanied by a glass of water. Water is, in effect, the country's national drink. It is always produced at mealtimes, with pastries, and with *ouzo*. In quite

Typical fishing boat

remote areas, water is even served together with wine or beer at table. The Greeks drink beer in the same way as they do wine. It is therefore possible to get several glasses of beer from one bottle. Yet getting drunk is simply not done. The Greeks enjoy getting mildly tipsy but drunkenness is considered utterly disgraceful.

The telephone often rings when the Greeks are sitting in the kafeníon. They use the telephone a great deal as it is very much cheaper than in Britain. They never give their name or the name of the company, hotel, etc. when answering a call. Instead the word '*Oríste*' is used, which does not indicate that everyone in modern-day Greece is named after the legendary hero Orestes, but means, quite simply, 'Hallo, can I help you?' Calls can be made within the local area from the kafeníon. Red coin-operated telephones are available everywhere for this purpose. These take two drachmas, and when a call has been made you should give another two drachmas to the landlord. With the high rate of inflation and ever-rising prices it is not worth converting the coin-operated telephones any more. The same can sometimes apply, although not very often, to the printing of bus and boat tickets. Often the conductor will quite legitimately demand an amount higher than the price printed on the ticket and the tourist incorrectly believes that he is being cheated.

After spending some time in the kafenío you may wish to pay a visit to the toilet; apart from in the best hotels, toilets are rarely like those at home. Soiled toilet paper has to be put in the waste bin or bucket provided and never into the lavatory itself as this can quickly block the drains.

You will never be left alone for long in the kafenío; someone will soon start a conversation. If something is then ordered for your new acquaintance, and the number of drinks has to be indicated by the fingers because your spoken Greek is not quite up to the task, the thumb is always turned into the palm of the hand. In Greece the thumb is only used when counting in complete sets of five.

Finally, some advice for women: a kafenío is really regarded as a man's place, and a foreign woman can sometimes find herself being eyed up and down as though she were a being from another planet!

In a kafenío

✕ Food and Drink

Greece can hardly be considered a paradise for gourmets but Greek cuisine does offer numerous dishes which are not very familiar to us in Britain. The main aim of the Hellenic cook is not to tickle the taste buds but to satisfy the guest's appetite and to provide his body with all the necessary nutrients, especially fat.

Food as a rule is not highly spiced and garlic is used far less than we think. There are two or three standard sauce recipes which are usually made from a base of tomatoes and olive oil.

Food sometimes comes to the table at a temperature which is gentle on the stomach, namely lukewarm. The reason for this is that most restaurants only cook once a day, usually in the mornings, and then, at best, the meals are kept warm throughout the day. If you like hot food it is best to arrive promptly at 12 noon, to order one of the numerous grills, or to say to the waiter *'polí sestó, parakaló'* (very hot please). If you are unable to get used to olive oil, then when ordering add the words *'me lígo ládhi, parakaló'* (just a little oil please) or *'chorís ládhi, parakaló'* (without oil please).

In the tourist centres there are many restaurants which cater for wider tastes and in the large hotels quite often it will be only the hors d'oeuvres which will remind you that you are in Greece. Very few language problems arise even in small restaurants and tavernas. If you are unable to read the menu, which does not always carry an English translation, then you may well be invited to go into the kitchen, as many Greeks do. Here you will find on a counter all the ready-cooked dishes and you can make your choice.

While hotel restaurants have fixed opening times, the majority of other bars and tavernas are open continuously from noon to midnight.

Ordering and paying

The term 'menu', meaning a set meal and not a bill of fare, is not understood by the Greeks. If you wish to order a meal in a restaurant which is not yet geared to tourists, then you must always ask for the dishes in the right order. Otherwise, everything will come to the table either all at the same time or else completely at random. When ordering, bear in mind that you will get a plateful of whatever you have asked for. If, for example, you order meat and two sorts of vegetables, three plates will be put in front of you. Usually only chips or noodles are served as an accompaniment to meat if nothing else is clearly shown on the menu. Throughout Greece it is customary to order portions of vegetables which are then shared between the whole group around the table.

A gathering around a table, *paréa*, has great significance in Greece. If you sit in a group, the cost is usually shared and it is unusual for bills to be requested on an individual basis. Whoever is paying must say *'tón logariasmó, parakaló'* (may I have the bill, please?).

Breakfast

Most Greeks do not have breakfast. They begin the day with a small cup of Greek coffee and during the course of the morning follow this with a rock-hard rusk *(paksimádi)*, fried eggs *(avgá mátya)*, or a bean soup *(fassoláda)*. As tourists like to

Dining at a taverna in Corfu

have breakfast, however, it is provided, although the Greeks' idea of breakfast is not the same as ours. There is hardly ever any fresh bread, but there might be some toast on the table. You might also get rusks, biscuits and a piece of plain cake, jam and butter. Coffee is often not served ready-made and has to be prepared by the guest from hot water and a coffee-bag. If you drink a particular brand of coffee, it is advisable to have some with you as it might not be available in Greece. Tea is almost always made with tea-bags and usually with warm water.

Boiled eggs are obtainable everywhere. An alternative to breakfast at a hotel is offered by the kafenía, confectioners' shops *(zacharoplastía)* and sometimes even by restaurants. There you can get, for example, *omelétta* (omelettes), *yaúrti me méli* (yoghurt with honey), *rizógalo* (rice pudding), *gála* (milk), and *gála sokoláta* (milk chocolate drink).

Aperitifs and hors d'oeuvres

The Greek national drink, *ouzo*, is commonly taken as an aperitif in some parts of Europe. The Greeks drink it as an accompaniment to a substantial snack of grilled *oktapódi* (octopus) or a plate of *pikilía* (hors d'oeuvres). Ouzo is an aniseed liqueur and flows crystal clear from the bottle but as soon as it is mixed with water it turns a milky white.

The most important of Greek hors d'oeuvres is salad which as *choriátiki* (peasant salad) is made of cucumber, tomatoes, peppers, olives, sheep's milk cheese, and sometimes capers. It is swimming in olive oil and comes to the table unmixed. Salt, pepper and yet more oil are placed on the table.

Other types of hors d'oeuvres (*oretiká* or *mesés*) are:

Sasíki	Salad made from yoghurt, grated cucumber, onions, olive oil and lots of garlic
Taramosaláta	Cold, reddish purée made from fish roes, moistened white bread or mashed potatoes, grated onions, salt and olive oil
Dolmadákia	Vine leaves filled with cold rice
Melisanosaláta	Cold puréed aubergines
Tirópitta	Sheep's milk cheese in a pocket of puff pastry
Spanakópitta	Spinach or mangel-wurzel in a pocket of puff pastry

Soups

Soups are rarely found on the menu in Greek restaurants, but in addition to the bean soup already mentioned in connection with breakfast, there are also:

Domatósoupa	Tomato soup
Psarósoupa	Fish broth (which does not have quite the same claim to fame as bouillabaisse)
Soúpa avgolémono	Broth with rice, eggs and lemon

Meat dishes

The belief of many Europeans that only lamb or mutton is eaten in Greece is quite unfounded. Generally speaking lamb is the most expensive meat and is usually imported from New Zealand. That is why beef and pork are more often found on the menu.

At all events, roast lamb is well worth trying and even if you do not particularly like mutton you have no need to worry. It is at the most only a year old and can hardly therefore be described as mutton. Moreover, the meat is almost always roasted over an open charcoal fire so that it has a most piquant taste.

In Greek, lamb is *arní* or (diminutive) *arnáki*; pork is *kirinó*; sucking pig, *gurunópulo*; beef, *moskári*; chicken, *kotópulo*; rabbit, *kunélli*. Meat is served as follows:

psitó	roast	*tú fúrnu*	baked	*vrastó*	boiled
kokkinistó	stewed	*skára*	grilled	*kimá*	minced

Souvlákia (singular: *souvláki*) are meat kebabs which are grilled on a hotplate or over an open charcoal fire. They consist of either pork or beef and are the favourite dish of many foreigners in Greece. On the other hand, only a few people enjoy *kokorétsi*, a sort of sausage made from offal, bound in a sheep's gut, and grilled over an open fire.

It is a speciality which can be found nowhere outside Greece, so for that reason pluck up courage and try it — just once, at least!

Fish and seafood

The Aegean is not well stocked with fish which is, therefore, expensive; it is only available on the coast and should be eaten only when very fresh. It is nevertheless quite tasty and the price is determined by weight.

Rénga	herring	*Skoumbrí*	mackerel	*Barboúnia*	red mullet
Ksifías	swordfish	*Glóssa*	sole	*Tónnos*	tuna
Astakós	lobster	*Oktapódi*	octopus	*Karavídes*	shellfish
Mídia	mussels	*Garídes*	scampi	*Kalamarákia*	squid

Pies and other delicacies

The Italian influence on Greek cuisine generally, including that in the Ionian islands, is reflected in the fact that the Greeks eat a lot of pasta. You will very quickly learn that spaghetti is referred to as *makarónia*. The true macaroni is only used in a sort of noodle pie called *pastítsio* which is prepared with mince and cheese. *Kitharákia* are a purely Greek speciality — pasta pieces the size of pearl barley; they are baked with beef in a dish known as *yuvétsi*. A famous pie is, of course, *moussaká* (see recipe).

Only seldom will you find *stifádo* on the menu. It is extremely delicious and is made from beef and onions in a sauce of olive oil, tomatoes and all sorts of seasonings which can range from cinnamon to caraway.

Stuffed vegetables are another speciality:

Domátes yemistés	Tomatoes stuffed with rice and mince
Piperiés yemistés	Peppers stuffed in the same way
Kolokíthia yemistá	Courgettes stuffed in the same way
Kolokíthakia yemistá	Zucchini leaves stuffed in the same way

Stuffed vine leaves are not only served cold as an hors d'oeuvre but also hot in a lemon sauce as *dolmádes*. Stuffed cabbage leaves are also served in a lemon sauce and are known as *lachanodolmádes*.

Desserts

Greek cheese is made from sheep's or goat's milk and its preparation varies from island to island. Only a slice is served and it is generally known as *fétta*. Apart from cheese, fruit (*frúta*) is the most commonly offered dessert in restaurants.

Mílo	apple	*Kerásia*	cherries	*Zíka*	figs
Stafília	grapes	*Peppóni*	honeydew melon	*Portokáli*	orange
Achládi	pear	*Fráules*	strawberries	*Karpoúsi*	water-melon

Coffee

Coffee was not originally served in restaurants and is only offered today in places which are frequented by large numbers of foreign tourists. Otherwise coffee may only be obtained in the *kafeníon* (café) or in the *zacharoplastíon* (confectioner's). Greek coffee (*kafés ellinikós*) is almost always served in little white coffee cups. It is always boiled up with the required amount of sugar; when ordering always state the degree of sweetness required, which of course is liable to be interpreted differently from one *kafen/on* to another.

skétto   unsweetened   *métrio*   semi-sweet   *glikó*   very sweet

Filter coffee is not available but instant coffee (referred to as *Nescafé*) can be obtained everywhere. It is served either hot or cold and when ordering you should indicate either *frappé* (cold) or *sestó* (hot).

Moussaká — a typical Greek dish

For four people: 1½ kg aubergines, 600 g minced beef, 2 finely grated onions, ¼ cup of vegetable fat, ½ cup of sweet vermouth, 500 g tomatoes, salt, pepper, ½ teaspoon of sugar, nutmeg or cinnamon, 3 dessertspoons finely chopped parsley, 6 dessertspoons flour, 2 beaten eggs, oil, 100 g grated Swiss cheese, 4 cups of béchamel sauce.

Wash the aubergines and cut into slices 1 cm thick. Add salt and leave to stand for one hour..Dry. Then fry until golden brown (for best results, do this the day before required). Fry the mince with the onions and pour in the wine. Add the peeled, thinly sliced tomatoes, salt, pepper, sugar, nutmeg, parsley and ½ cup water. Simmer for 45 minutes; allow to cool and add flour, eggs and some of the cheese. Arrange a layer of aubergines in an oven-proof dish and sprinkle with cheese. Spread the mince over, put the rest of the aubergines on top and sprinkle again with cheese. Cover with a thick layer of béchamel sauce. Bake at a moderate temperature for 1-1¼ hours.

Cakes and pastries

Pastries (*gliká*) clearly reveal their oriental origin: they are all very sweet and inclined to be fattening. Nevertheless you should try:

Báklava   Flaky pastry filled with sugar, almonds and other nuts, and drip-
                   ping with honey.
Galatópitta   Semolina cakes filled with vanilla cream.
Loukoumádes   A kind of doughnut filled with a honey and sesame sauce.

Drinks

Tap water, ice cold, is almost the Greek national drink. It is called *neró*, can be safely drunk everywhere, and costs nothing.

Beer (*bíra*) is now quite often available on draught as well as in bottles. The only traditional Greek brand is-called *Fix*, and its sales have suffered by imports from foreign breweries.

Wine (*krassí*) is produced on all the islands but is not often available by the glass or carafe. Bottled wine, however, is good value. The best-known Greek wine is without doubt *retsína*, a white wine flavoured with the resin collected from the Aleppo pine. It originated as a result of practical necessity. The ancient Greeks had neither bottles nor watertight barrels and transported their wine in goat-skins or large clay vessels which were coated with pine resin in order to seal them; this also prevented a second fermentation. The practical necessity no longer exists but the Greeks do not wish to abandon the taste of the resin!

Shopping

The majority of Greeks appear to be born salesmen. Before tourists came to the country there was very little evidence of this, but since the advent of mass tourism everyone who had an eye to business opened a souvenir shop. The choice shows very little imagination as everyone sells exactly the same things as his neighbour. If you keep your eyes open, however, you might come across something interesting among all the trinkets on display.

Carvings from olive wood are certainly worth considering. The wood is put in store for about four years to season before the wood carver begins his work. His ability and the quality of the wood determine the price. The best wood comes from young branches but both the trunk and the boughs are also used.

Pottery is produced in many places in Greece. In addition to the copies of painted antique vases, the many creations by young potters, mostly from Athens and Sifnos, enjoy great popularity.

The tanning of **leather** took place on the Ionian islands until just a few years ago. However, because of the smells created, which were not very pleasant, it is now considered preferable to leave this process to the modern tanneries on the mainland, and the islanders restrict themselves to the manufacture of bags, shoes and all sorts of accessories from imported hides.

Woven, knitted and embroidered goods come mostly from other regions in Greece, but hand-made goods are produced on the islands by many women, young and old alike. Their best items are often found in *Eommex* shops which are situated on almost all of the Ionian islands. Eommex is the Greek organisation for small and average-sized industries.

Gold and silver jewellery is usually better value than in Britain, the reasons being lower wages and smaller profit margins.

Genuine classical antiques and icons on the other hand are not souvenirs and their export is strictly forbidden. The penalties for unsuccessful attempts at getting them out of the country are high. Those who like them must make do with copies, which are on sale everywhere. Icons are best purchased where the local people buy theirs: in shops which specialise in church interior decoration.

Natural products and island specialities. Souvenirs which are cheaper than, and at least as original as, man-made handicrafts are those which nature has produced. A jar of olives from the Ionian islands is undoubtedly a typical present; fresh almonds and pistachios will also please someone at home. Records or cassettes of Greek music will later revive holiday memories and if you wish to dance to them you can buy an appropriate recording which comes complete with instruction book.

Kumquats, orange-coloured fruits from a small tree which came originally from China, are a Corfiot speciality. The 3–5-cm-long fruits are candied and used for making jam or liqueur.

Toilet water and aftershave lotion are manufactured on Corfu, and also on Zákinthos where strawberry liqueur, *halva* and *sisami* are additional specialities.

Shopping in Corfu town

Halva is a hard dessert made from almonds, honey or sugar, water and milk; sisami is a bar made from sesame seeds and honey, and is convenient as travel rations for walkers.

On Lefkás you can sample and buy home-produced banana, peppermint and cherry liqueur. In addition, local makes of *ouzo* and brandy are on sale. The brandy tastes quite different from *metaxa* which we tend to think of as the typical Greek brandy.

A good wine to take home with you, in spite of its weight, is produced on Cefalonia. Dry, white *robola* comes in bottles which are packed in attractively presented sacking material.

Just a word about prices: haggling is virtually non-existent now in Greece. Only when buying relatively expensive goods is it worth while making a cautious, polite try.

Hints for your holiday

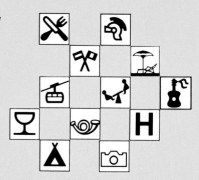

Xéni or pelátes?

Until only recently hospitality was considered to be an inherent quality of the Greek people. Twenty years ago both guests and foreigners were described by the same Greek word *xénos*, but today the majority of foreigners, *xéni* (plural), are looked upon as *pelátes* (customers) by the local people. The behaviour of many tourists is unfortunately much to blame for this.

In order to know how to behave in a manner expected of visitors you must first learn something about the customs of your hosts. Bathing attire should only be worn on the beach. Anyone who goes into town wearing a bikini, bathing trunks or tight shorts will be considered very improperly dressed by the Greeks, who would also think that only a thoughtless heathen would go into a church or a monastery with bare thighs or shoulders. If you wish to visit a monastery or convent, do not disturb the monks or nuns during the period between 1 and 4 o'clock, and if a church is specially opened for you to visit it, leave a small donation in the offertory box. The Greeks are very proud of their past. No stone, not even an insignificant-looking fragment, may be removed from an archaeological site as this is looked upon as theft. Possession of and trading in drugs are dealt with very severely indeed.

If you wish to photograph people, first obtain their permission. In the place of words a smile will always do. Most of all, never let the lack of a foreign language stand in the way of politeness. Those who cannot say '*parakaló*' or '*efkharistó*' can get by with 'please' or 'thank you', and if you cannot remember the Greek expressions for 'good morning', 'good day' and 'good evening', you can simply say '*yassú*' at any time of the day or night, as it can mean 'hallo', 'goodbye' and even 'cheers'.

It is really quite easy to make friends with the Greeks. If he wants to find them hospitable, the visitor has only to behave as a considerate guest.

Corfu harbour

Where to go and what to see
Corfu (Kérkira)

Corfu makes its living from the tourist industry. With over 300,000 foreign visitors per year, it takes third place behind Rhodes and Crete among the 200 inhabited Greek islands. The majority of tourists come from Britain, with the Greeks themselves in second place, followed by the Germans. Yet Corfu is not even half the size of Rhodes and is almost fourteen times smaller than Crete. It is roughly the same size as the Spanish island of Ibiza.

What makes Corfu so popular is its excellent combination of climate and character. In summer it is always pleasantly cooler by some degrees than the Aegean and in winter it rains so much that plant life can thrive even in the hotter months. The rainfall has turned Corfu into one of the most verdant islands in Greece. The 3.5 million, mostly very old, gnarled olive trees contribute greatly to the character of this island, and they themselves result from a significant aspect of Corfu's past. Unlike all the other Greek islands (except Paxos) Corfu was never ruled by Turkey. Whereas the rest of mainland Greece was for centuries burdened with the Turkish yoke, and even the other Ionian islands lived under the Turkish flag for several years at least, or indeed decades, it was the Venetians who were the masters on Corfu. A glint of their splendour and wealth rubbed off on the Corfiot aristocracy, leaving its mark on the lifestyle of a small section of the upper class. It was the Venetians who forced the Corfiots to cultivate plantations of olive trees, and the Venetians who, together with the local nobility, put their architectural stamp upon the character of the old town of Corfu (Kérkira), which still has something of an Italian air.

A further influence on the look of the town came from the French during the period of the Napoleonic Wars. The British also bequeathed numerous buildings during the first half of the 19th c., until 1864 when Corfu was finally united with independent Greece, fifty years earlier than Crete and eighty-three years earlier than Rhodes. There is therefore much in Corfu which looks familiar to us by comparison with southern Greece, just as life in general here is a little less alien to us.

Corfu has an above-average range of good hotels and a wide choice of bars and restaurants catering for foreign visitors. With its many excellent beaches, which are situated mainly on the west and north coasts, and its numerous opportunities for water sports, the island meets all the principal requirements of its guests. In addition, the various types of scenery on Corfu are very impressive. The barren, rocky Pantokrator (906 m) dominates the north; the last stretch of the journey to its peak is over hazardous little roads, but there is a wonderful view over the whole island and across to Albania. In the central and southern part of the island wooded hills alternate with olive-covered plains, rugged, steep coasts with concealed bays, smooth lagoons with romantic river courses. In spite of the many holidaymakers there is still much to be discovered off the beaten track: tiny churches and decaying forts, little monasteries and isolated beaches, and ruins from Greek and Roman antiquity, completely overgrown by vegetation.

Corfu town *(Kérkira)* Pop. 37,000

In the best holiday tradition, you can enjoy sightseeing, shopping and relaxing at leisure in pleasant street cafés in this town. Corfu town is worth more than just one visit.

📷 Places of interest in the town

(The figures in brackets refer to the plan on page 29.)

Around the Esplanade

The large open square between the old town and the fortress is known by the Greeks as *Spianáda* (Esplanade). Many houses stood here until well into the 16th c. In 1537, however, when the Turks first laid siege to Corfu's fortifications, the Venetians had the whole of this part of the town demolished. They wished to leave the besiegers with no cover and to create an open field of fire for themselves. After the Turks had been driven off, the Venetians used the Esplanade as an exercise ground. Today it is the social centre of the town where everyone meets, and an especially popular place for an evening stroll, a *volta*. All the important processions and rallies take place here.

The Esplanade is divided into two parts by Dousmani Street; in the northern part during the summer months a game is played here which is to be found nowhere else in Greece – cricket, a relic from the time of the British Protectorate. The club has a certain amount of difficulty in finding opponents, as these have to come from Great Britain, Australia or New Zealand, but a few international matches are played each year. Otherwise the club fields two teams of its own.

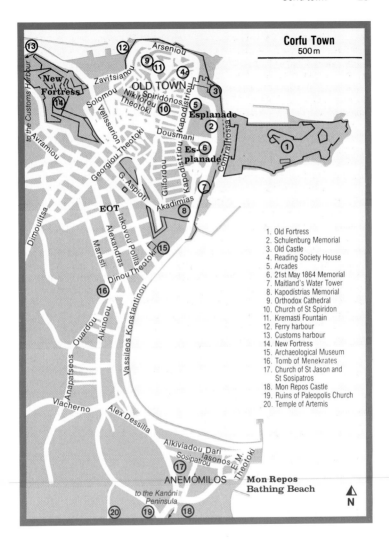

Corfu Town
500 m

1. Old Fortress
2. Schulenburg Memorial
3. Old Castle
4. Reading Society House
5. Arcades
6. 21st May 1864 Memorial
7. Maitland's Water Tower
8. Kapodistrias Memorial
9. Orthodox Cathedral
10. Church of St Spiridon
11. Kremasti Fountain
12. Ferry harbour
13. Customs harbour
14. New Fortress
15. Archaeological Museum
16. Tomb of Menekrates
17. Church of St Jason and St Sosipatros
18. Mon Repos Castle
19. Ruins of Paleopolis Church
20. Temple of Artemis

The Old Fortress (1) *(Paleo Frourio)*. The fortress which lies on a promontory is reached by crossing a small bridge over the *Contrafossa*, a straight moat filled with seawater, and dug by the Venetians in the 16th c. to give further protection to the building. Today fishing boats and pleasure craft are moored here.

The peninsula on which the fortification stands is overlooked by a hill which has two peaks, 51 m and 65 m in height. These two prominent peaks gave

The Contrafossa

their name to the whole of the island: *korypho* means peak, and from the plural *koriphi* the word Corfu was later derived by the Venetians.

Although this promontory has had defences and houses on it since the 6th c., almost all the buildings which remain date from the British period. Parts of the old walls have crumbled through weaknesses in their construction and other parts were blown sky-high when two massive explosions occurred in the powder magazine in 1718 and 1789. During the Second World War German bombs caused further damage.

In addition to the huge walls and bastions, *Ágios Georgios* (Church of St George) is worth a visit. It was built by the British in 1830 as a garrison chapel in the style of a Doric temple. A climb up to one of the twin peaks on the peninsula would also be worth while as there is a wonderful view from the top over the town and the island. Unfortunately the climb is sometimes prohibited for military reasons.

The Schulenburg Memorial (2) stands at the entrance to the Old Fortress on the edge of the Esplanade. It is a memorial in honour of Count Johann Matthias von der Schulenburg, a German who in 1716 successfully defended the island for the Venetians against the besieging Turks. The fact that it was erected during his lifetime (in 1716, in fact) was a special honour seldom bestowed upon anyone by the Venetian Republic.

The Old Castle (3), also known as the *Palace of St Michael and St George*, blocks off the northern end of the Esplanade. Built between 1816 and 1823, it was originally intended as the residence of the Lord High Commissioner; it was named after the two saints as it was also the home of the Order of St Michael and St George. This order of knighthood was founded at the same time as the palace was built, in order to honour British officers who had faithfully served the Crown in Malta and the Ionian islands.

The British nation was wealthy then. Yellow limestone was imported from Malta for use as a building material and the façade of the palace was graced with twenty Doric pillars. As a finishing touch, a Corfiot sculptor created a frieze depicting the emblems of the other Ionian islands: the head of Odysseus for Ithaca, Aphrodite rising from the waves for Kýthira, and the trident for Paxos. The emblem of Corfu, the prow of a ship, crowns the frieze.

Part of the old castle's interior is open to the public; of the former staterooms the dining room, the throne room and a circular ante-room are preserved. The remaining suite of rooms on the first floor is given over to a *museum* with two quite different departments. In one, Byzantine frescos, mosaics, fragments of buildings and icons are displayed; in the other, there are examples of Asian art. This came to Corfu because the government did not know what else to do with it when a Greek diplomat donated his collection to the nation in 1919.

Reading Society and Rotary Club (4). This establishment is evidence, as is so much else, of the British influence on the island. Despite its library of 30,000 volumes the Reading Society, founded in 1836, is more like an English club.

The Arcades (5) with their cafés and restaurants, on the other hand, will remind you of Paris. They were built when Baron Mathieu de Lesseps was the French governor of the island. He did not live to see the completion of the work begun in 1807 as it took fifteen years. Lesseps based the Corfiot arcades exactly on those he had erected in the Rue de Rivoli in Paris only a short time previously. However, a building project by his son, Ferdinand de Lesseps,

The Palace of St Michael and St George

earned far greater fame than did the Arcades in Corfu, for his son was the builder of the Suez Canal.

The Memorial of May 21st 1864 (6) commemorates the day on which the Ionian islands were united with independent Greece. Just as in the frieze on the façade of the Old Castle, the emblems of the seven largest Ionian islands are represented.

Maitland's Water Tower (7), which looks like an Ionic rotunda (*tholos*) and could also be described as colonnaded, is actually a work from the last century, a memorial to Sir Thomas Maitland, the first Lord High Commissioner of the Ionian islands. During his term of office (1816–1824) the town of Corfu was given a modern water supply system and rather fittingly the rotunda was built over a cistern of that period.

The Kapodístrias Memorial (8) was erected in memory of the first leader of independent Greece, Yánnis Kapodístrias, who held office between 1827 and 1831 and was born on the island of Corfu.

The Orthodox Cathedral of Panagía Spiliótissa (9). A visit to the cathedral is well worth while, if only to see its valuable icons which date from the 15th and 16th c. The relics of St Theodora are preserved in a silver casket which is on view in a side chapel. The 9th c. Byzantine empress is revered as it was she who reintroduced icons into the Orthodox Church following the iconoclastic controversy, when their worship was fiercely debated. The 16th c. cathedral which has an 18th c. Baroque façade was badly damaged by German bombs during the last war but was later painstakingly restored.

The Campiello Quarter (the Old Town)

To the north-west the Esplanade joins up with the network of narrow alleyways of the Old Town which still bears its Italian name of Campiello. This is where the Italian influence is most noticeable. Completely untypical of Greece are, for example, the multi-storeyed dwellings dating from the 17th and 18th c. in each of which live several families. The shopping arcades on the ground floor of the buildings in the main street are also typical of Venetian architecture. In summer the arcades provide shade and in the winter they give protection from the rain.

Numerous tiny 17th and 18th c. churches are scattered all over the Old Town. They are kept closed nowadays and are only opened when a mass is being celebrated, as so many art treasures have been stolen from Greek churches over the years.

The Church of St Spiridon (*Ágios Spiridonos*) (10). This church on the main street, Odós Spiridónos, is an exception, however; it is the most important church in the town and is open to the public. Its particular significance derives from the fact that the bones of St Spiridon are preserved here in a silver casket and are worshipped by the local people. With a single nave, the church was built at the end of the 16th c. and has the highest bell-tower on the island.

St Spiridon lived during the 4th c., at first as a shepherd but later as a bishop on the island of Cyprus. In the last years of his life he performed several miracles and as a result he was canonised shortly afterwards. When his remains were exhumed after several decades they were found to be completely intact. In the 7th c. they were removed to Constantinople. A short time before the city was taken by the Turks in 1453, a priest took the remains to northern Greece where they were finally purchased as a relic by a rich Corfiot family. According to popular belief St Spiridon performed numerous further miracles on Corfu. The four most significant are celebrated annually by colourful processions through the town. In the 15th c. he delivered the island from famine; in 1630, and again in 1673, he brought a great plague to an end; and in 1716 in the opinion of the people of Corfu he assisted Count Schulenburg in beating off the Turks. Many precious candelabra and lanterns inside the church reflect the gratitude felt by the faithful in return for the performance of many small, personal miracles. The twenty paintings on the ceiling are by the 19th c. Corfiot artist, Nikólas Aspiótis, and the icons, some of them very valuable, are by various 17th c. masters.

The Kremasti Fountain (11) which stands in the midst of the maze of tiny alleyways of the Old Town is a fine example of Venetian fountain construction. A nobleman, Antonius Cocchinus, had it erected in 1699, as the Latin and Greek inscription says, 'for the well-being of the people'.

At the Harbour

The Ferry Harbour (12) is the second most important social centre on Corfu, after the Esplanade. The oldest hotels in the town stand around the harbour square, and restaurants and cafés place tables and chairs outside under the clear, blue sky. Horse-drawn carriages await their rich, romantic passengers, and it is from here that ferries sail to Igoumenítsa, Paxos and Patras – there is always plenty of activity.

The Customs Harbour (13) is by comparison modern and dreary. It has one function only — the ferries which travel to and from Italy are handled here.

The New Fortress (*Neo Frourio*) (14), which is really not so new, stands south

Corfu town

of the ferry harbour. It is the counterpart of the Old Fortress and work was begun on it by the Venetians in 1572. The purpose of this fortress, which formed part of a whole series of new ramparts and bastions, remains of which may still be seen in the town today, was to help protect Corfu against Turkish invasion or siege attacks. Only part of the New Fortress may be viewed as it is still used by the Greek Navy.

In the south of the town

The Archaeological Museum (15) contains all the finds which archaeologists have made on Corfu during the last 150 years. The finest specimen in the collection is the famous *Gorgon Pediment* of the Temple of Artemis which was erected in the ancient town of Corcyra. It was unearthed shortly before the First World War by German archaeologists and was described in a scientific article by Kaiser Wilhelm II. In the Lion Room between the entrance hall and the Gorgon Room is the sculpture of a reclining lion which was discovered close to the tomb of Menekrates. It is even older than the sculptures of the Gorgon relief and dates from the 7th c. B.C. In the same room you can see pieces from the roof of an ancient temple on which some hint of colour is still preserved; an indication that the fine marble of the temples built in Classical times was originally brightly painted. On view in the two remaining rooms are numerous other sculptures, ancient coins, architectural fragments, reliefs, pottery and work fashioned from bronze.

🖼 The Gorgon Pediment in the Archaeological Museum of Corfu

The Gorgon Pediment of the Temple of Artemis which was built in the ancient town of Corcyra is the most important archaeological discovery on the Ionian islands. It is the only example of Archaic pediment sculpture dating back to the very earliest years of Classical Greek art. It was created in the period around 590 B.C. by sculptors from Corinth, where the formal language of the Classical Doric temple was being developed at that time. However, as no similar works from this period have been preserved in Corinth itself, the pediment sculptures of Corfu have a special value. The figures are exceptionally well preserved and where pieces were missing archaeologists have indicated them carefully and in clear distinction from the original, so that the observer gets a complete understanding of the piece.

In the centre of the 2.7-m-high pediment is Medusa, represented in the running position characteristic of the Archaic period. Medusa was the mortal sister of the two Gorgons who lived beyond the ocean. Whoever looked her in the eyes was immediately turned to stone. The hero Perseus beheaded Medusa with the help of the goddess Athena, who from that time on carried her head as a fearful weapon on her shield. Offspring sired by Poseidon who came to life from the Medusa's dying blood were the winged stallion Pegasus, and a son called Chrysaor. The small, now legless and one-armed figure to the right of Medusa is taken to be Chrysaor. To the left, the tail and hindquarters of Pegasus are clearly recognisable. Two fabulous creatures, lion-like imaginary figures, flank Medusa on both sides. The small figures behind these creatures represent the Greek gods in battle against the Titans, from whom they seized power in order to be able to set themselves up as rulers on Mount Olympos. To the left, Poseidon is pointing his spear at Kronos, the father and forerunner of Zeus, Poseidon and Hades; to the right, Zeus himself is slaying a Titan.

The portrayal of these battles may be seen as an indication of the honour accorded to all the Greek gods. The two lions identify Medusa as the mistress of animals, a role which in former times she shared with Artemis to whom the temple is dedicated. The head of Medusa interwoven with snakes is designed to ward off demons and other evil spirits from the temple, a not unimportant task in times when demons were so greatly feared, as they were until the Classical period at least.

The Tomb of Menekrates (16) which is situated in the yard of a police station dates from the period around 600 B.C. The area in which it stands was in ancient times a cemetery serving the town of Corcyra.

The St Jason and St Sosipatros Church (*Ágios Iásonos kai Sosipátros*) (17), in the suburb of Anemómilos, is one of the few churches on the Ionian islands which have been preserved from the mid-Byzantine period; that is from the centuries prior to the conquest of Constantinople by the Crusaders in 1204. It was built about the year 1000 A.D. Typical of such churches are the ground plan, which is in the 'inscribed cross' style of Greek architecture, the dome, which in this case rests on an eight-sided drum, and the ante-room or narthex which extends in front of the actual church, and was originally used for the reception of worshippers who were not yet baptised. In the church you can still see fragments of old wall paintings and icons from the 17th and 18th c.

Castle of Mon Repos (18) **Paleopolis Church** (19) and the **Temple of Artemis** (20). Leaving Corfu town and heading southwards towards the Kanóni Peninsula you come to a cross-roads, to the left of which lies the Castle of Mon Repos which, however, is not open to the public. Built in 1831 as a summer residence for the British High Commissioner, it later became the property of the Greek royal family following independence. Prince Philip, Duke of Edinburgh, was born here in 1921. In the castle grounds, which are also private, archaeologists have discovered the ruins of several ancient temples.

The impressive ruins of the Paleopolis Church stand opposite the entrance to Mon Repos. As long ago as the 2nd or 1st c. B.C. the Romans built a small music theatre or odeon here. The early Christians erected on the same site a mighty five-aisled basilica. In later centuries this place of worship was constantly being destroyed and rebuilt until bombs brought about its final ruin in 1940.

If you walk on from here for about 10 minutes, you will come to one of the most romantic spots on Corfu, the *Convent of Ayi Theodori* (Ágii Theódori) and the sparse remains of the Temple of Artemis. Proceed along the road leading from the church ruins and then turn left to the rear of a huge building which looks somewhat like a school (the Olive Research Institute of Corfu). Apart from during the midday break, the nuns are always pleased to accompany visitors through the convent chapel to the library where several icons from the 17th and 18th c. are on display. The foundation walls of the temple — the only remains — lie in an enclosed but accessible area to the right below the convent gate. It is now only possible to make out the external dimensions. The ancient building was some 47 m long and 22 m wide and was, like the Parthenon on the Acropolis at Athens, surrounded by eight pillars across its breadth and seventeen pillars along its length.

If you walk just a short distance from the convent, you will soon come to a particularly well preserved section of the ancient city wall or, to be more precise, to a part of a wall tower. Because a small chapel had been built into this tower in the 11th c. this part of the wall was not plundered for building material in the same way that so many other ancient buildings were during the Middle Ages.

In addition to the museums already mentioned, there are others in the town catering for more specialised interests: the *Museum of Byzantine Art* in the Antivouniótissa Church in Odós Arséniou, the *Museum of Paper Money* in the Ionian Bank building in the Platía Iróon Kipriakoú Agónos, and the *Sólomos Museum* in Odós Arséniou which houses works by writers from Zákinthos.

Averof, homely little taverna behind the Hotel Acropole at the ferry harbour, with an extraordinarily large selection of unusual Greek specialities; *Bella Vista*, a restaurant with an unparalleled view, beneath the Achilleion Palace on the road to Benítses (some 9 km south of Corfu town), with a large number of fish dishes but with meat also available; *O Pontis*, a taverna which lies outside the town on the road to the Achilleion Palace where barbecued *kokorétsi*, lamb and goat are served each evening; *Yannis Taverna*, a plain, traditional taverna in the suburb of Anemómilos, Odós Sosípatros 43.

Solemn processions on the *Feast Days of St Spiridon*: on Palm Sunday, Easter Saturday, August 11th and the first Sunday in November. *The Corfu Festival* in September with performances by visiting members of international theatre, ballet and opera companies and orchestras.

🎸 Displays of folk dancing in the Old Fortress daily from May 15th to September 30th (apart from during the full moon), followed immediately by a *son et lumière* display on the history of Corfu.

♣ Roulette, Chemin de Fer and Black Jack in the casino situated in the *Achilleion Palace*. A bus which is free of charge runs from the Ferry Harbour, Esplanade and Corfu Palace Hotel to the casino. Jackets and ties must be worn.

🛵 Numerous moped and scooter hire firms.

♘ Riding stable at the *Kérkira Golf Hotel*. Horse-drawn carriage drives from the Esplanade and Ferry Harbour.

🚴 In the *Corfu Hilton* on the Kanóni peninsula.

⛳ *Corfu Golf and Country Club*, an 18-hole course in the *Rópa* valley, 16 km beyond the town.

🎾 At several hotels and at the *Corfu Tennis Club*, Odós Romanáu 4; Squash at the *Corcyra Beach Hotel*.

🏊 🤿 There are no fine beaches in Corfu town. You may swim either in the open-air baths at the *Nautical Club* situated beneath the Old Fortress or in the small beach pool at *Mon Repos* to the south of Corfu in the suburb of Anemómilos.

⛴ Several times daily to *Igoumenítsa* on the mainland; once or twice a day to *Paxos*; several times weekly to *Ithaca, Cefalonia* and *Patras* as well as to various Yugoslav ports; in addition, daily trips to several Italian ports.

ℹ️ *Greek Tourist Information Office (EOT)* in the administrative building on Diikitírion Square.

🚌 Excursions from Corfu town

The Kanóni Peninsula, the islands of Vlachérna and Pontikoníssi (4 km)

The view from the top of the Kanóni Peninsula over the two little islands of Vlachérna and Pontikoníssi (Mouse Island), as well as over the eastern coast of Corfu which lies beyond them, is so well known that it is chosen as the cover picture for many books written about Corfu. There are two large terrace cafés here which will tempt you to linger awhile. The peninsula has been called Kanóni ever since the French installed a cannon here, on the top, to defend the entrance to the Chalikópoulos lagoon. During the present century the Greeks have built the runway for the Corfu International Airport here; it actually stretches out into this lagoon. In addition to the lovely scenery you can now see aircraft roaring past so close that it seems you can almost touch them. Yet no damage seems to have been done to the romantic setting.

You reach the island of Vlachérna by crossing a causeway. The island is completely paved over, and on it stands a tiny convent where two or three (very camera-shy) nuns still live. The 17th c. building is architecturally and artistically uninteresting but a visit just for the atmosphere generated there is highly recommended.

From the causeway to the island of Vlachérna you can take a trip in a motor boat to the islet of Pontikoníssi just two minutes away. Nobody knows why it is called Mouse Island. Nestling between the cypress trees and other greenery is a tiny little church, the date of which is variously given as the 11th or the 19th c! A series of marble plaques commemorates royal visits. If you have no time or enthusiasm to make the trip here, don't worry, as the view from Kanóni across to the island is much more rewarding than Mouse Island itself.

Kanóni — Vlachérna and Pontikoníssi islands

Pérama, 7 km from Corfu town, is connected to the Kanóni Peninsula by a causeway for pedestrians and cyclists which also carries a water main. If you stop for a rest on one of the viewing terraces you can see Mouse Island from a different angle and also watch the aircraft landing.

 Yannis Restaurant is chiefly a fish restaurant, and is situated on a terrace overlooking the sea; very atmospheric. *Panorama* is a cosy little place on a terrace facing Mouse Island, for those with only a small appetite — or just a thirst.

 Pedal boats which may also be taken across to Mouse Island.

Kaiser's Bridge is a memorial set in the water on the coastal road: Kaiser Wilhelm II's landing stage is situated beneath his Achilleion Palace. Four rusty bollards manufactured long ago in Vienna, two marble dolphins and a rather dilapidated bit of masonry are all that remain.

The Achilleion Palace (Akhíllion)

The Achilleion situated 9 km from Corfu town above the east coast is probably Corfu's most visited tourist attraction. Empress Elisabeth of Austria had it built in 1892 in the Classical style by an Italian architect. Corfu lay only a short distance away by sea from the then Austrian dependencies of Dalmatia. Elisabeth, born in 1837, the daughter of the Bavarian Duke Maximilian Josef, married the Austrian Emperor Franz Josef I in the year 1854. In 1861 she visited Corfu and immediately fell in love with the island. Thirty years later the palace was built. From then on the empress spent a few weeks here twice a year until her murder by an Italian anarchist in Geneva in 1898. Following her death the Achilleion stood empty for eleven years until it was bought by the German Kaiser, Wilhelm II. He had only a few alterations made and retained its name. Just like the empress the Kaiser was also an ardent admirer of the Homeric hero Achilles. China, silver cutlery, and almost every household utensil in the palace were decorated with dolphin heads. Dolphins are seen as the sacred animal of Thetis, the mother of Achilles. In the lovely palace grounds each of the two owners erected a monumental statue of the hero which reflected their different temperaments — Elisabeth's was of the dying Achilles and Wilhelm's showed the 'Victorious Achilles'.

When the First World War broke out in 1914 Corfu's period as the summer residence of German-speaking rulers finally came to an end. The Achilleion was used as a military hospital and numerous pieces of furniture disappeared. The same thing happened during the last war. A gaming casino was opened in the palace in 1962 and life began again for the Achilleion. Part of the income earned from the casino was directed towards restoration and the repurchase of pieces of furniture which

had previously been pilfered.

On the ground floor of the palace you can view some of the Kaiser's private rooms, as well as the tiny palace chapel and the entrance hall with its huge ceiling-painting depicting the four seasons. In a modest museum room is the chair in the form of a saddle on which Wilhelm used to sit while working at his desk, as well as a model of the SS *Hohenzollern*. Until 1914 the Kaiser used to take his spring cruises on this ship. A schedule for one of the cruises hangs on the wall. Only a small part of the beautiful park is open to the public — the upper terrace of the palace with the two statues of Achilles.

Northern Corfu

Gouviá

Situated 9 km to the north of Corfu town, Gouviá, which lies on a sheltered bay in a charming part of the countryside, is the second seaside resort on the east coast, after Kontókali. It was here in the 18th c. that the Venetians built a huge shipyard where repair work was carried out and where ships spent the winter months 'in moth-balls'. Walls, columns and archways may still be seen but the roof is missing. These ruins are reached by taking the old road to Gouviá and at the town sign taking the road which leads down to the sea (roughly 200 m).

Dafníla — The Village

From a distance Dafníla appears to be the most delightful village on Corfu, nestling cosily among the dense foliage. But it is an artificial village. The Corfiot brothers Bouas, who made their money from tourism, built it in order to create a new tourist attraction. Historically styled buildings stand along the main street which is about 100 m long. There is an authentic village church and a platía

The Achilleion Palace

Looking towards Gouviá from Kontókali

with a kafeníon. Masses of tables and chairs are placed nearby, and in the evenings over a drink and something to eat, holidaymakers can sit and enjoy performances of Greek folk-music recitals and other forms of entertainment.

It really is worth a visit but 'The Village' hardly has an air of Greece about it. Nowhere can you get ouzo with mesé (aniseed liqueur with tasty snacks) which would otherwise be served in every little village taverna. However, there is a pub with the typically Greek name of 'The Marquess of Queensbury'! The first drive-in cinema in the Ionian islands is the Bouas brothers' most recent achievement and is situated close to Dafníla.

Dafníla (The Village)

Dasiá

This coastal village, 12 km from Corfu town, offers some of the best sporting facilities in Corfu. Like all the others on the east coast the beach is only one or two metres wide; because of this the hotels have a lot of space for sunbathing and there are wooden bathing platforms built out into the sea. Dasiá is also the 'clubbing' centre on the island. The Robinson Club can be found in the south of the village and the Club Méditerranée in the north. Both clubs have excellent sports and amusement facilities.

    Parasailing.

   Pedal boats.

Ípsos, 15 km from Corfu town, immediately adjoins Dasiá and is very popular with campers.

Ágios Márkos

A little way inland lies Ágios Márkos which for art-lovers is well worth a visit. Above the village, quite clearly to be seen from the main street, stands the small *Church of the Pantokrator* (ruler of the world). Built in 1576, it contains many well preserved wall paintings from that period which mainly portray saints and events from the New Testament. Outside, the walls of a monastery to which the church presumably used to belong are gradually falling into decay.

A second, very much older church (11th c.), also containing well preserved frescos, is situated half an hour away below the village, in an olive grove. It is called *Ágios Merkoúrios* but is, unfortunately, kept locked.

From Ípsos to Kassiópi

A twisting road winds up the hillside overlooking the sea, which at this point looks more like an inland lake as the Albanian coast is so close. Short detours will take you to beautiful beaches and dreamy hamlets. Old and modern houses, occupied mainly by British holidaymakers, may be seen everywhere among the olive groves.

Barbáti is the name of a long pebbly beach as well as being a small village with a fortified tower. This was built to provide protection against attacks by marauding pirates.

Kalámi is a lovely little bay enclosed by cypress trees, with very few houses or tavernas. The author Lawrence Durrell once lived in the three-storeyed white building and it was here that he wrote his book about Corfu, 'Prospero's Cell'.

    Parasailing.

Kouloúra, set amid particularly lush vegetation, lies on the small bay adjoining Kalámi. At the end of the main street there is a 16th c. fortified manor house which is, unfortunately, not open to the public.

   Boats for hire.

  Boats for hire.

Kassiópi, 36 km from Corfu town, is a busy seaside resort on the north coast very close to the Albanian shore. The town was of importance during Roman times as every ship bound for Italy waited here until favourable winds permitted the crossing of the Ionian Sea. Cicero and the Emperor Nero both spent some time here, in 48 B.C. and 67 A.D. respectively. Where at that time there was a temple dedicated to Jupiter, there stands today the *Church of the Panagía*

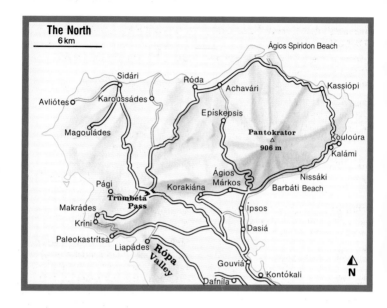

The North
6 km

Ágios Spiridon Beach

Sidári
Róda
Achavári
Kassiópi

Avliótes
Karoussádes
Epískepsis

Magouládes
Pantokrator
△
906 m
Kouloúra
Kalámi

Pági
Korakiána
Ágios Márkos
Nissáki
Barbáti Beach

Makrádes
Trumbéta Pass
Ípsos

Krini
Dasiá

Paleokastrítsa
Liapádes
Rópa Valley
Gouviá
Kontókali
Dafnila

N

Kassopítra which contains 17th c. frescos and precious icons from the 16th to 18th c. The exterior is also very interesting as the priest's house is actually built over the church.

On a hill overlooking the town you can see the almost completely overgrown outer walls of a huge castle. It was built in the 12th c. and was destroyed by the Venetians in 1386. Lying below this castle are the town's two most beautiful coves.

Three Brothers, a large restaurant situated on the platía with fresh fish and roast lamb in garlic as specialities. *Kassiópi Star*, a modern restaurant, specialising in shrimps with ham.

The best beaches lie to the west of the town beneath the medieval castle, ten minutes' walk from the platía.

Pedal boats for hire.

Excursion to the Pantokrator

Another way to get from Ípsos to Kassiópi is via Epískepsis. The journey on this road is well worth while if you wish to have an outing to the top of the Pantokrator, the highest mountain on Corfu (906 m). A poor road leads almost up to the peak on which stands a 13th or 14th c. monastery, now in ruins. Each year on August 6th it becomes a place of pilgrimage. The view over Corfu and out towards Albania is breathtaking. To the north you can see the tiny islands of Othoní, Erikoussa and Mathráki, and in the south you can see Paxos. On some days the view even extends as far as Lefkás.

The north coast from Kassiópi to Sidári

Some of the island's finest beaches and coves can be found on this stretch of the coast.

Ágios Spiridon is the first you come to; it lies a little way off the main road and has two tavernas and 100 m of the finest sand.

      Pedal boats, canoes.

     Parasailing.

Achavári is a vast holiday development with an extensive sandy beach stretching as far as *Róda*.

      Pedal boats, canoes.

A Special Tip

Occasionally trips to the lonely islands of Othoní and Erikoussa may be arranged from the harbours on the north coast. The main occupation on the islands is lobster fishing, and fresh lobster is therefore a dish on the menu of all the islands' tavernas.

Sidári has sandy beaches which stretch for miles. You can soon find your own small cove which has been carved out of the rocks by the sea. The low cliff coastline is very colourful around here and the rocks are so soft that curious formations have been sculpted by the sea. One of these, known as the *Canal d'Amour*, is a passage worn through an outcrop of rock. According to local superstition an unmarried girl has only to wade through this passage thinking of the man of her dreams and the banns can be put up!

     Canal d'Amour, the oldest restaurant in Sidári, with a large

choice of dishes, especially fresh fish.

      Pedal boats, canoes.

        Parasailing.

From the north coast to Paleokastrítsa

From Sidári the road leads high up into the mountains to the *Trumbéta Pass*. There is a magnificent view from here. One of the most lovely and still relatively little-used roads on the island leads from the pass via Makrádes to Paleokastrítsa.

Makrádes is one of the most traditional villages on the island and it is enjoyable just to stroll around it at leisure. At every opportunity the local people try to tempt you with very reasonably priced almonds, wine, oregano, craft work, and lodgings for the night in their own homes — something which very rarely happens elsewhere on Corfu.

If you go down from Makrádes to the neighbouring village of *Kríni* and walk for about 25 minutes along a lane, you will come to the foot of the 300-m-high, steep rock face of a hill on top of which stands the old Byzantine castle of *Angelókastro*. Built in the 12th c., the castle played an important role in the defence of the island until the 18th c. Today it is a romantic place for walkers and nature-lovers alike. From the castle of Angelókastro walk on further for 1¼ hours and you will come to Paleokastrítsa.

Paleokastrítsa, 25 km from Corfu town, lies on and around a number of tiny bays, verdant promontories and steep slopes densely covered in vegetation, and is considered by many to be the island's most beautiful town. It is no wonder that there are many more hotels and guest houses here than there

Paleokastrítsa Bay

are ordinary, traditional town dwellings.

In addition to the scenic panorama over the area, the town's second attraction is the Monastery of *Kímesis tou Theotókou* (Repose of the Virgin). It is situated on a 60-m-high hill which can be reached by car and on which,

Bell-tower of the Monastery of Kímesis tou Theotókou

according to some archaeologists, the palace of Alkinoos could have stood in Homeric times or even earlier. The monastery's setting, its sparkling whiteness and its idyllic covered walkways all add to its special charm. Some splendid icons hang in the monastery chapel, including over the entrance a 17th c. representation of the Last Judgment. In the museum is a visitors' book in which entries were made on April 22nd 1909 by Kaiser Wilhelm II and Oscar, Prince of Prussia. On show in a display case is a bible dating from the 13th c. when the monastery was founded. The buildings which are still intact, however, date from the 18th and 19th c.

    Pedal boats and canoes.

   Barracuda Diving School.

A Special Tip

You can enjoy one of the finest panoramic views in the world from the café terraces in *Lakones*, a tiny village perched on the side of the hill above Paleokastrítsa.

The beach at Érmones

Beaches to the south of Paleokastrítsa (see map page 39)

Instead of driving direct to Corfu town from Paleokastrítsa, you can take another route through the fertile *Rópa Valley* with its well tended golf course. By doing so, you will get to know a few more beaches and a charming little hill town.

Érmones, about 20 km to the south of Paleokastrítsa, is a bay dominated by an unconventional, terraced, large beach hotel. As the coastline is so steep at this point the hotel has its own cableway which runs from the road to the beach below. Legend has it that Odysseus was washed up on this beach after being shipwrecked for the last time during his wanderings. Nausicaa, the daughter of the Phaeacian king Alkinoos, who lived in Paleokastrítsa, found Odysseus there and took him to her father's palace where he was asked to tell the story of his adventures. Alkinoos then provided Odysseus with a ship so that he could finally return to his homeland of Ithaca.

The beach of Mirtiótissa can only be reached after a difficult climb down the sheer cliff face but it is well worth the effort. Overlooking the beach stands the *Panagía Mirtiótissa Monastery* which was founded in the 14th c. by a Turk who had been converted to Christianity. The present buildings, however, are all of recent date.

The beach of Glifáda is altogether much easier to get to. Overlooking the beach is the hill village of Pélekas, a holiday resort much favoured by young visitors. The summit of the hill is appropriately named 'The Kaiser's Throne' as the German Emperor Wilhelm II often drove to this point in his red Mercedes to see the magnificent sunsets over the island.

The southern part of the island

Benítses

You can still see the remains of a Roman bath in this former fishing village which lies 13 km from Corfu town. If you follow a path leading from the back of the small square for about 50 m you will come to the thickly overgrown walls which once surrounded the private bath-house of a Roman villa. The *mosaiká* (mosaics) are unfortunately no longer to be seen as they have been covered with sand and earth to protect them from further damage.

 Narrow stretch of beach right by the coastal road.

Moraítika

A few remains of a Roman villa may be seen here too. Like Benítses, Moraítika is chiefly a lively seaside resort, and as it is situated near the mouth of the Messongi river, nature-lovers will be particularly attracted to this area.

 Yoanna restaurant, intimate, rustic, good value.

  Pedal boats, canoes.

Messongi is the village on the other side of the estuary, hidden away in an olive grove on the water's edge.

Lefkímmi

The little Potámos river flows through the eastern end of this large attractive village built along a single street and situated 40 km from Corfu town. The view from the bridge looking across to the fishing

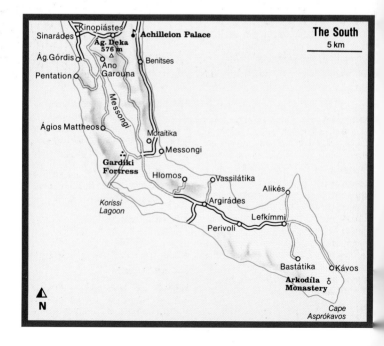

Benítses

boats, the cottages and the cypress trees on the river bank is very attractive. A detour will take you to *Alikés* on the coast where, apart from a good beach, there is also a large area of salt workings.

  Church festival on July 8th.

Kávos

In this most southerly resort on the island, 47 km from Corfu town, the beach is unusually wide and long for this stretch of the coastline. Accommodation is provided only in small guest houses and private apartments.

 On foot, by car or on horseback to the abandoned monastery of *Panagía Arkodíla* (approx. 4 km) and then a further 4 km on foot or on horseback to *Cape Asprókavos*, the southernmost point of the island.

 The beach at *Cape Asprókavos* where the sardine fishermen set sail can only be reached by boat.

   Parasailing.

The interior of the island and the west coast

Gardiki. If you return along the western side of the island in the direction of Corfu town, you will see on a slight mound right by the road a Byzantine fortress which dates from the 13th c. Its external walls and towers are extremely well preserved but the interior is a romantic, lonely little spot, completely overgrown with lush vegetation. Not many people come here.

A signposted road leading from the fortress will take you further away from civilisation to the *Korissí Lagoon*. Unfortunately the sandy banks of the lagoon will prove a disappointment. Bathing in the lake is not permitted and there is only an unattractive stony beach on the sea-shore on the other side of the narrow tongue of land. However, it is worth making the detour just for the peace and quiet of the area.

Áno Garoúna is the sort of hill village you find in picture books. It is situated on the lower slopes of the highest mountain in the southern part of the island, the 576-m-high Ágia Déka. Donkeys and mules are still the most important means of transport and more local people than foreigners frequent the kafenía.

Ágios Górdis is ranked among the most attractive places on the island because of its scenery. It also has one of the sandiest beaches. Bizarre rock formations which create a splendid backdrop and small rocks on the beach catch the eye. Numerous tavernas provide refreshment.

Excursions to the mainland

If you wish to take the opportunity of crossing over from Corfu and getting to know something about a relatively obscure part of the Greek mainland, then you will have to make your own arrangements and hire a car, as organised tours of this kind are not often available. Nevertheless it is worth it. A two-day excursion would, of course, be preferable to a one-day trip, as you have to allow a good 1½ hours each way for the crossing.

Igoumenítsa, the port on the mainland, is very much a commercial town which does not have a great deal worth seeing. There is however a frequent bus service from here to Ioánnina which is 104 km away by well maintained road.

Ioánnina Pop. 40,000

The capital of the northern Greek region of Epíros lies on the bank of a huge lagoon between high mountains and has an eastern air about it. In the Old Town you can still see two *mosques* with minarets, as well as a genuine *Turkish bath*. A very good *archaeological museum* stands in the main boulevard, the Leofóros Averóf.

A boat trip on the lake to an island surrounded by reeds, known simply as *Níssi* (island), is particularly fascinating. There are several churches and monasteries here with well preserved wall paintings, and also a small museum with memorabilia from the end of Ali Pasha's reign of terror. It was he who at the beginning of the 19th c. wrested Epíros from the sovereignty of the Turkish Sultan.

Xenía, one of the best guest houses in Ioánnina; *Palládion*, *Espería*, *Olympic*, *Galaxy*.

The stalactite caves of Pérama

Situated 4 km from Ioánnina, these caves are among the largest and most splendid in Greece. The lighting is very effective, and the round tour (total distance 1 km) is an experience not to be missed.

Dodóna, which lies 21 km to the south-west of Ioánnina, is one huge archaeological site where the ancient Greeks used to worship Zeus, the father of the gods. Particularly well preserved is the large theatre from the period around 200 B.C., built to accommodate 18,000 spectators.

Paxos (Paxi)

Many of the tiny Greek islands have suffered the same fate as Paxos: up to a few years ago they were dormant almost the whole year round, and they still are apart from in the holiday season. Then they are overrun with crowds of tourists who come to Paxos because they have picked it out as a small, possibly quite peaceful, secluded and unspoilt island. There are probably more visitors here relative to the total population than there are on Corfu, although at present there is only one hotel of any size. Most holidaymakers stay either in private accommodation or in old houses which have been extended or modified and are probably run by British tour operators.

Provided you are not under the impression that you will have the island to yourself, you will find it an extremely charming place. Life in each of the three coastal townships is concentrated into a very small area and generates a friendly and intimate atmosphere in which the visitor quickly feels at home. Other islands have a large number of olive groves; Paxos is almost one single forest of olive trees. Old farmhouses, tiny churches and endless drystone walls and terraces are tucked away among the trees, and walks in the shade are a great pleasure. World history has not left its mark on Paxos, so the scenery, nature and tourist life in the coastal villages are the only things to tempt visitors to this island.

Gáios

Gáios (Pop. 400)

The island capital, where car ferries and passenger ships tie up, lies on a bay which seems to be almost completely taken up by the island of Ágios Nikólaus. This island, covered with pine trees of various kinds, is so close to the coastline of Gáios that the open sea is generally not visible and it is easy to believe that you are on the bank of a river. Elegant yachts and small open motor boats ply up and down this 'river'. Each evening large fishing smacks tow a line of tiny fishing boats out to sea past the visitors, who sit in the cafés on the platía of Gáios as though at the theatre.

The many multi-storeyed stone houses reflect the affluence of their owners. The most splendid building in Gáios is the former British Residency dating from the 19th c. It is situated on the waterfront and is now used by the harbour police. At the other end of the promenade is the memorial to Geórgios Anemoyánnes, who set fire to a Turkish ship in the harbour at Paxos during the Greek War of Independence (1821-1829).

 Blue Grotto grill; *Anesis* confectionery shop which serves *loukoumádes* in the afternoons.

🎵 *Castello.*

🚲 Bicycles, mopeds and motor scooters (no driving licence necessary).

🌊 Gáios itself does not have a beach. If you wish to bathe you can either drive or walk to the other resorts on the island. Alternatively, there is a regular hourly crossing by motorboat to the Moggonísos Peninsula in the south of the island, where there is a beach of sand and shingle set in perfect surroundings.

⛵ 🛶 Motorboats (no driving licence required).

 Connections with Corfu, Ithaca, Cefalonia and Patras.

⚓ Connections with Párga on the mainland.

Longós is the smallest of the three fishing villages on Paxos and the shore of its small semicircular bay is bordered by perhaps thirty houses, mostly two-storeyed. Behind the town dense olive groves cover the gentle slopes of the hill. A few small fishing boats bob up and down in the water at the quayside

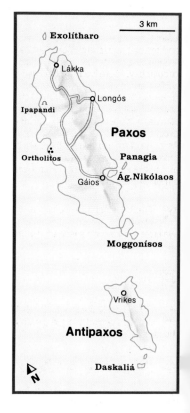

opposite the many kafenía and tavernas, which are somewhat simpler and more traditional than those in Gáios. On the edge of the village can be seen a large dilapidated factory building where olive oil was pressed years ago.

 Rocky and shingle beach 5 minutes to the south.

 Greek Islands Club.

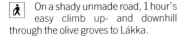 On a shady unmade road, 1 hour's easy climb up- and downhill through the olive groves to Lákka.

Lákka, on the northern coast of Paxos, and facing the island of Corfu, extends around the inner end of an almost circular bay. There is a British-run wind-surfing and sailing school here and in summer the water is alive with the colourful sails of yachts. The slopes on all sides are covered not, as you would expect, by olive trees but by cypresses. As in the other two villages there are no more than a few dozen houses in Lákka, all built along the sea-shore and with only a few little streets behind.

 Fresh lobsters are served at the *Nautilus*. These are always available from a cage suspended in the sea right in front of the restaurant.

 Aloni.

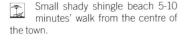 Small shady shingle beach 5-10 minutes' walk from the centre of the town.

 Connection with Corfu.

Cave on Paxos

A Special Tip

The almost completely enclosed bay of Lákka is ideal for windsurfing. Even in the strongest wind it is quite safe for competent practitioners of the sport. It is an excellent place for beginners to learn.

 Excursions

Circular tours of the island by boat

Circular tours by boat may be made from all three coastal resorts. The west coast of the island with its steep cliffs is particularly impressive. You can occasionally watch monk seals in the numerous caves. The *Ipapandi* cave is supposed to have been the hiding place of a Greek submarine during the Second World War. The tour boats go into the *Petriti* cave where a spectacular play of light and colour greets you, as in the

Rocky outcrops at Párga

Blue Grotto of Capri. The *Ortholitos*, a magnificent obelisk of rock, and the arch of *Tripito* are remarkable rock formations.

Antipaxos (Andípaxi)

Just 2½ km separate Paxos from its tiny sister island of Antipaxos. It is not the olive which predominates here but the vine; wine and cereals are the island's main products. Antipaxos supports about a hundred people, but this population is not geared to tourism. Those hardy folk who wish to spend a night on the island generally sleep on the beach. The white sandy beach of *Vríkes* is considered the best on the island and every visitor enthuses over the crystal-clear water. A small taverna on the beach provides simple refreshment.

Párga

This little port on Greece's northern coastline in the region of Epíros lies opposite the island of Paxos. Its houses nestle on gentle slopes which overlook a delightful bay. The green of the groves of olive, lemon and orange trees forms a wonderful contrast to the blue sea and the red roofs of the buildings which are very much in the style of the mainland. A place that is worth visiting is the massive *Venetian castle* in the north of the town, built about 1570.

To the residents of the Ionian islands, Párga is chiefly a symbol of the injustice of British rule. In 1815 the British delivered the town into the hands of the Turkish tyrant Ali Pasha from Ioánnina who had for years tried without success to take the town by force. Many Greeks who had earlier fled to Párga to escape the Turks had to leave once more and the majority of them sought refuge in the Ionian islands, where a handful of their descendants live to this day.

Houses in Párga

By boat around Paxos

Lefkás (Lefkáda, Leukas)

A channel only 40 m wide separates the island of Lefkás from the Greek mainland. Whether this channel has always existed is much debated. We do know that the ancient writers Polybios, Livy and Strabo were all of the firm opinion that it had been created by the Corinthians and that previously Lefkás had been just a peninsula forming part of the Akarnanian landscape.

That is quite possible. Between Lefkás and the mainland stretches a unique area of lagoons and marshes, almost completely closed off in the north by a narrow tongue of land 1 km long. Perhaps it was the Corinthians who cut their way through this spit, in order to save their ships, which in those days were very small, from having to sail round the island on the far more dangerous seaward side. Nowadays a swing-bridge has replaced two antiquated chain-ferries which used to travel back and forth, day and night, continuously ferrying people, cattle, buses, lorries and cars. On the Lefkás side one road leads across the spit to the island capital on the lagoon, and another goes over an artificial causeway built by the English. As you look across the lagoon from the island side, the hills of the mainland are always within view. In fact those who spend their holiday here will have the feeling of being on a huge lake not dissimilar to those of northern Italy. On the west coast of the island, however, you will get a completely different impression. Lefkás is bordered on that side by a 34-km stretch of steep cliffs falling sheer into the open sea. There is not a single harbour on this coastline. A chain of mountains, the highest of which is Stavrótas (1141 m), cuts through the middle of the island.

Its proximity to the mainland has not always been exactly advantageous for Lefkás. It came under Turkish rule three times during the course of its history, one period lasting 181 years from 1503-1684. Fortune, however, was on the side of the islanders in 1953 when a massive earthquake destroyed the majority of buildings on other islands in the south of the Ionian chain. Only very few houses here were damaged. The Lefkadians still used the old building method, perhaps inherited from the Turks, of constructing the upper floors of their houses from wood. For that reason many of these old houses are still standing on Lefkás today, whereas on the other islands modern buildings have been erected which have far less character.

Lefkás town

The island's capital is bordered by the lagoon on three sides and was established in 1445 on a sandy spit of land which had all the necessary requirements for a safe harbour.

Through the middle of the town runs the main street, the eastern end of which is named after the German archaeologist Wilhelm Dörpfeld, but which for the rest of its length is called Zákka Street. It has an eastern air about it, as many of the houses in the road are apparently built of wood, although in fact móre and more wooden walls are being ripped down and replaced by almost identical-looking synthetic materials. Fortunately this has not affected the atmosphere of the town. The majority of the capital's shops can be found in this street. In the evening the people of Lefkás come here for a stroll, and they invariably pause in one of the street cafés or restaurants situated at either end of Dörpfeld Street. The noise often lasts until midnight but nobody worries, because practically everyone is out there anyway, or playing with their children in the large playground down by the harbour, which really only becomes busy after nightfall.

The most important churches in the town are to be found in the main street. They all date from the 17th or 18th c. and are more Venetian than Greek in appearance. On the outside they are graced by magnificent doorways but are otherwise quite unpretentious and simple. Their bell-towers were all destroyed by the earthquake of 1953 but shortly afterwards makeshift ones made of iron were put up, and these are still there today. Apart from during services the churches remain locked. The interior decoration is almost exclusively Ionian Baroque, and is thus reminiscent of western European models.

The two museums in the town are of little more than local importance. In the *Archaeological Museum* (Odós Faneroméni 21), which consists of only one room, have a look at the four urns on the wall facing you, on the left, as they are very interesting. They are still filled with ashes, and if the museum attendant is in a good mood he will raise the lid for you and let you look inside — something which is not normally permitted. The second museum in Lefkás is the *Laografikó Mousío* (Folk Museum) which contains memorabilia of life on the island in years gone by. It was established by one of the arts societies which play a very important part in the social life of the island.

 Romantica, a garden restaurant in a side street off the Odós Zákka. Here you will sit surrounded by sweet-smelling blossoms, and trees with bird cages hanging from their branches. The sound of Greek music being played will take you far away from the hustle and bustle of the main street. A speciality not often found is served here: *lachanópitta* (spinach and mint in puff pastry). *Specialist No 1, Pete Vlachos*: the owner of this restaurant which is situated in the middle of the hubbub of Dörpfeld Street

considers himself a souvlaki specialist (see page 21) — and he really is. *O Krinos*, a kafeníon in the Odós Zákka opposite the police station, is decorated inside in an old-fashioned style with a lot of pictures, photographs and mirrors on the walls; here you will find Greeks playing cards and tavli. Food is not obtainable here but drinks are decidedly cheap.

      Aravanis, Brumis

 A handicraft shop which has no name and is situated in the old Hotel Averoff on Dörpfeld Street sells extremely tasteful items such as hand-painted plaques, modern artistic ceramics, and copies of works by Theofilos painted on aged wood. Theofilos (1868–1934) is Greece's greatest 'naive' painter.

 At least 1 km beyond the town, on the sand-spit.

An international *festival of folk dancing* is held during the second half of August.

Excursions from Lefkás town

The fortress of Ágia Mávra

The walls of a massive fortress, the Ágia Mávra, rise up on the mainland side of the sand-spit at the point where the channel cuts through it. The fortress is normally locked but the key may be obtained from the small kafeníon next to the bridge. The inside of the fortress is today one big yet romantic wilderness. Old Venetian cannon barrels lie scattered around in the tall grass and steps lead nowhere. The tiny 18th c. *Church of Ágia Mávra* and the old prison are really all that remains intact, but the view over the countryside from the outer walls is splendid. You can see right over

The fortress of Ágia Mávra

the lagoon to the town, over the channel to the very fine beach on the sand-spit, to the mainland, and to the nearby Turkish *Tekla Castle* which dates from the 17th c. The Ágia Mávra fortress itself goes back as far as A.D. 1300 but was extended and restored by the Venetians in 1684.

Church festival in honour of St Mávra on May 3rd.

Excursion by boat to Meganísi

Probably the best trip from Lefkás town is to the little island of Meganísi which is largely untouched by tourism. People will look at you in amazement and certainly with a smile on their faces if you ask for a hotel or private room. After all, why pay out money when you can sleep under the stars for nothing? Meganísi, just 18 sq. km in area and with a population of just over 2000, is the ideal place for lovers of nature. The 4.2-km-long road links the three island towns of Vathí (where the excursion boats from Lefkás tie up), Katoméri, and Spartochóri, but thus makes only a small part of the island accessible. Meganísi is shaped like a Greek gamma and though quite narrow is fairly long — an eldorado for those who enjoy walking through unspoilt and undeveloped countryside. If you go looking for sandy or shingle beaches, you will be disappointed as the shores of this island are rocky. You will probably wish you had more time than a one-day trip from Lefkás town allows, for you may find you spend all of it in one of the kafenía at the harbour in Vathí, with the romantic view of the deep, bottle-shaped bay and over the gently rolling, green hills. While there, you will also perhaps notice that the best site in the town, that is at the very end of the bay, is occupied by a children's playground and not, as might be expected, by a hotel.

Apart from four private rooms there is no other indoor accommodation available. In spite of the Greek laws regarding casual camping, sleeping under canvas is possible anywhere on the island.

On Meganísi

By bus to Aktion and Nikopolis (about 26 km)

The name Aktion recalls a crucial event in Roman history, the naval battle of Actium fought on September 2nd in the year 31 B.C. Following Caesar's murder, the sovereignty of the Roman Empire was shared by two powerful men, Octavian, who later became the Emperor Augustus, and Antony whom of course we associate with Cleopatra, Queen of Egypt. In the naval battle of Actium the 500-strong fleet of Antony and Cleopatra was defeated by Octavian's 250 ships. At an early stage and without real cause, first the queen and then her Roman ally fled from the scene. Antony's land forces surrendered after waiting in vain for about a week for their general to appear. The man who was later to become the Emperor Augustus immediately set about building a large new city which he called Nikopolis, 'City of Victory', on the place where his camp had been. For many Greeks this was a defeat; they had to leave their home towns and move to Octavian's new city whether they wanted to or not. That also happened to the majority of the people of Lefkás.

In Aktion (about 20 km from Lefkás town) all that is to be seen today is a small Venetian-Turkish fort. What took place there in Roman times must be reconstructed in the imagination.

On the northern side of the entrance to the Gulf of Ambrakia lies the little town of *Préveza,* which is linked to Aktion by a car ferry operating throughout the day (the crossing takes 10 minutes).

Six kilometres from Préveza, standing on both sides of the road to Arta, are the still impressive ruins of Nikopolis which was finally abandoned in the 13th c. The remains of the city wall, the theatre and several basilicas from the Byzantine period (5th–6th c.) may still be seen.

Circular tour of the island

Heading south along the coastal road on the eastern side of the island, 2 km beyond Lefkás town, you pass the small hamlet of *Kaligóni.* In ancient times, the island's capital was situated behind this village on a slight hill covered with olive trees, to the right of the road. If you climb the hill and wander around among the trees, you can still find a few remains of the city wall, built of polygonal stones which in a few places still stand 4-5 m high. The road now leads past some tiny coves where you can swim, and after 17 km reaches the village of Nídri.

Nídri

After Lefkás town, Nídri is the most important holiday resort on the island, and the majority of holidaymakers here are British. The beach is long and narrow. Almost all the tavernas and kafenía place their tables and chairs outside, right on the quay. The view is outstanding: to the south *Vlichou Bay* cuts deeply into the land and is crowded with the colourful sails of the wind-surfers, and on the far side of the entrance to the bay an obelisk, erected by the Greeks in honour of the German archaeologist Wilhelm Dörpfeld (1853–1940), rises from the green knoll of *Ágia Kiriakí,* opposite the church of the same name. Dörpfeld had a villa here given to him in 1907 by Kaiser Wilhelm II, and he is also buried here. The islanders respect him particularly because he was persuaded that Lefkás was the Homeric Ithaca, the home of Odysseus, and he endeavoured to prove this theory — which nevertheless turned out to be false — in several academic publications. Dörpfeld was also of the opinion that Nídri was the site of the palace of Odysseus.

There is more scenic beauty to be viewed from Nídri. To the east are several small islands lying close to the

Nídri

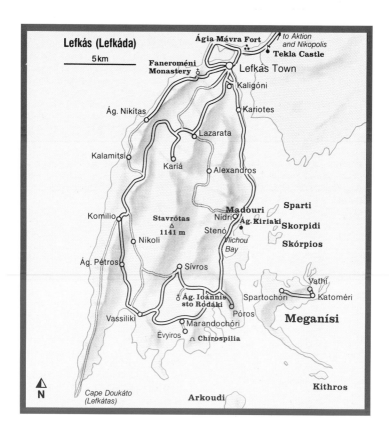

Nídri

coast, some of which are privately owned by quite well known people. The islet of *Madouri* belongs to the Lefkadian family of Valaoritis whose most famous son was the poet Aristoteles Valaoritis (1824–1879). His romantic works celebrated the fighters of the Greek War of Independence, and he himself supported the union of the Ionian islands with an independent Greece. The villa built by the poet in the Classical style can be clearly seen from Nídri.

The second private island off Nídri, the famous *Skórpios,* is owned by the heirs of the shipping magnate Aristotle Onassis. The extensive lawns are still tended and the flood-lighting over the tennis courts is still turned on quite often. But the harbour and the private beaches on the island are mostly deserted nowadays and helicopters rarely land on the strips which were specially built for them. The property is patrolled by guards, however, who ensure that no unauthorised person sets foot on this unusually lush island.

 Motor boats bring tourists to Ágia Kiriakí and close to the shores of the private islands of Madouri and Skórpios.

On both sides of the road as you leave the town of Nídri there is an enclosed stretch of land known as *Stenó.* The fence is there to protect Dörpfeld's excavation site, the only one remaining on Lefkás. There are thirty-three circular graves here, each with a diameter of anything up to 9 m, and each originally surrounded with limestone slabs about a metre high and covered with earth to form the shape of a cone. Dörpfeld believed these to be royal graves from the time of Odysseus but modern archaeologists are of the opinion that they are about 800 years older, dating back to the early Bronze Age.

Póros

Póros, 27 km from Lefkás town, is situated on a hill overlooking Rouda Bay which has a superb beach and is reached by taking a small road out of the town. The *Análipsis* church in Póros itself is worth a visit as it contains some frescos which date from the 18th c. If you walk for about five minutes from the church you will come to the remains of a watch tower from the Hellenistic period (4th c. B.C). 7-m-high fragments are still standing. The tower was probably built to protect an olive press.

There are two possible routes for the journey to *Vassilikí*: the road fairly close to the coast, via Marandochóri, or the one which takes you inland via Sívros. By taking this road you will come to a signposted lane which branches off to the left shortly before you reach Sívros. This leads to the *Monastery of Ágios Ioánnis sto Rodáki*, which however is only of special appeal to those interested in archaeology, for the 18th c. monastery buildings are in ruins. There is very little left of the ancient temple which once stood here but some parts of it have been incorporated into the walls of the monastery buildings. According to Dörpfeld this temple would have been larger than the Theseion in Athens or the Temple of Poseidon at Cape Sounion on the Attic mainland.

It is also possible to reach a place of historical interest from the other road: the *cave of Chirospilia*, five minutes' walk to the south of the village of Évyiros. It was here that Dörpfeld discovered tools and pottery from the late Neolithic Age (around 2000 B.C.). The name of the cave suggests that pigs were kept here for many centuries. Dörpfeld assumed therefore that the farmstead of the swineherd Eumaeus who is mentioned in the 'Odyssey' was also quite close to the cave.

Vassilikí

Vassilikí, 38 km from Lefkás town, is as beautiful as any other place on the island. The small harbour basin, full of colourful fishing boats, is surrounded by eucalyptus trees under which stand tables and chairs from the numerous quayside tavernas and kafenía. The upper storeys of many houses, like those of the island capital, are made of wood, corrugated iron or synthetic materials, giving an unusual atmosphere to the town. There are, however, no other sights of particular interest here.

 A white beach of sand and shingle, with no shade, about 1 km long, immediately north-west of the harbour.

 Pedal boat hire.

Boat trips to the steep cliff coast of Cape Lefkátas (Doukáto) may be arranged.

Leaving the fertile plain of Vassilikí with its orchards, olive groves and vineyards, the road climbs upwards to the large village of *Ágios Pétros* where the women still often dress in traditional Lefkadian costume. The Venetian-style outfit is usually of dark blue or bottle green.

In Komílio, to the north of Ágios Pétros, a road branches off in a southerly direction taking the visitor to the barren *Lefkátas peninsula* which is generally deserted. It ends after roughly 20 km at the cape of the same name, which is also known as *Cape Doukáto* or *Sappho's Leap*.

Cape Lefkátas

A temple of Apollo stood here in ancient times and Dörpfeld deduced that it must have been sited exactly under the present-day lighthouse. This temple was the centre of a cult which, over 2000 years ago, attracted followers and curious onlookers from the entire Greek world every year to its ceremonies. For priests and criminals leapt into the sea from the steep cliffs which at this point rise to a height of 70 m. Wings and even birds were fastened to their clothing in the belief that the fluttering of the birds' wings would lessen the impact with the water. Fishing boats waited beneath the cliffs with nets spread ready to rescue those lucky enough to survive the leap. The priests returned to Lefkás and the wrong-doers, who were now considered free, were safely escorted to a place of exile. Apollo was not only the god of light but also the god of atonement, and this strange custom must have had something to do with this fact. Perhaps there is also a connection with the custom of recording on the wall of the Temple of Apollo in Delphi the names of all slaves allowed to go free.

This cape is also named Sappho's Leap because it was here, according to later belief, that the poetess Sappho, suffering from a broken heart, is supposed to have cast herself into the sea. This is highly unlikely, however, as this first great lyric poetess of world literature (7th c. B.C.) lived on the island of Lesbos which is a long way away in the northern Aegean.

For the journey back to Lefkás town there are two possible routes: along the coastal road or through the hilly interior of the island. The highest point on the coastal road is the little development of Ágios Nikítas on the north-west coast.

Ágios Nikítas

In the summer, this little fishing village (12 km before you get to Lefkás town) is completely given over to tourism. The beach, stretching out in front of the village which consists mainly of tavernas and car parks, is not particularly good, but a little way to the north-east there is a 2½-km-long beach of coarse light-coloured sand and shingle. Its impressive position at the foot of the mountains makes up for the fact that the beach is completely without shade.

 Pedal boat hire.

If you travel along the coastal road, you will pass the *Faneroméni Monastery* where the view over Lefkás town, the lagoon, and the Akarnanian mainland opposite is particularly attractive. The inland road winds its way through barren hill country, the bleak character of which is broken up here and there by a few young cypress trees and some isolated vineyards.

Kariá

The hill village of Kariá will take you by surprise with its magnificent square, the platía. You can sit there for hours in the shade of age-old trees, drinking ouzo or coffee and sampling all sorts of choice morsels. Even today, women still fetch water from the well in the square, while in the steep alleyways of the village women sit knitting, embroidering, and making pillow lace. From time to time, practice pieces performed by the 'Apollo' music society resound through the village — the Greece of days gone by still lives on here.

A Special Tip

A festival in honour of St Spiridon is held in Kariá from August 11th to 13th, when many villagers wear their traditional costume.

On the return journey to Lefkás town there is an opportunity to make a detour to the half-ruined monastery of the *Panagía Odoyítria* founded in 1450. The church, which is unfortunately locked most of the time, is the only surviving place of worship on the island from the period prior to the conquest of Constantinople by the Turks. The restored wall paintings inside the church date from the 15th c.

Ithaca (Itháki)

Ithaca is the island to choose if you enjoy walking. You should head for the sites of Homer's 'Odyssey' which every local will be able to point out to you. The enthrallingly beautiful but by no means gentle landscape through which you pass is as rewarding as the legendary places themselves. It is best to walk on Ithaca as the buses operate on only a few routes and do not run very often. Tour buses and hire cars are not available at all. You can hire mopeds, but because of the considerable gradients on some parts of the island they often prove more trouble than they are worth. Taxis do exist, but because of the bad roads they are unable to take you to all the places worth visiting.

What makes Ithaca's scenery so delightful is the constant interplay between steep cliff coastlines, deeply cut bays, barren or scrub-covered hillsides, green olive groves, and magnificent views over Ithaca and the neighbouring island of Cefalonia, as well as the ever present sea. Life in the modern towns has been little influenced by tourism; there are few good beaches.

Vathí Pop. 2500

The island's capital, as its name suggests (see page 94), lies at the inner end of a deeply curved bay and has no view out to the open sea. The platía, on the quay, is the centre of the town and here the tourist can find everything for his daily needs: travel agency, post office, banks, cafés and restaurants.

If you take a stroll through the long, narrow town an old villa on the esplanade to the east of the platía will catch your eye. It is the only house which came through the earthquake of 1953 unscathed. Take a look at the Orthodox Cathedral (Mitrópolis), dedicated to the Presentation of Mary in the Temple, which has a beautiful wooden screen. The town's little archaeological museum has been closed for years, but the memorial to the poet Lord Byron, in an adjacent garden, is freely accessible. Byron was on the island in August 1823, nine months before he died of malaria, in April 1824, in Messolóngi on the Greek mainland. His enthusiasm for Ithaca was so great that he wrote the lines which today appear on his memorial: 'If this island belonged to me, I would bury all my books here and never go away'.

The islet of Lazaretto, only a very short distance from Vathí, was where Byron went to swim every morning. During the period of the British Protectorate, the island became a quarantine station; hence its name.

 Restaurant Momo; Psitaría Nea Itháki, on the shore (kokorétsi a speciality).

 Loutsa on the eastern shore of the bay of Vathí, 30 minutes away on foot. Boat shuttle service to Vathí in the summer.

 Pedal boat hire on Loutsa beach.

Eommex sales kiosk on the platía.

Celebrations during the evening of August 15th (Repose of the Virgin).

Connections once daily with Astakós on the mainland and with Sámi and Ágia Efímia on Cefalonia.

A Special Tip

Every year in July a music festival takes place in Vathí to which well known Greek and foreign artists are invited. Míkis Theodorákis is often here as a guest.

In the summer boat trips may be made once daily to Kióni in the north of the island.

In the area around Vathí

Sarakinikó: a walk of 1¼ hours on a good path.

In 1979 a group of Germans of every age, who had become bored with their life at home, purchased an area of land here of over 720,000 sq. m with almost 700 olive trees on it, in order to put into practice their ideas of an alternative way of life. If you would like to witness this experiment at first hand, then apply in writing to Sarakinikó before setting out on the trip and you will be made welcome. The isolated beach on the Bay of Sarakinikó also makes the short hike worth while.

Arethusa's Fountain *(Aréthousa Kriní):* a two-hour walk, first on a good path, then on a stony mule track; signposted.

Odysseus' swineherd, Eumaeus, is supposed to have watered his pigs daily at this fountain which bears the name of a legendary water-nymph. This is rather difficult to imagine, as the fountain lies at the end of a steep narrow gorge hemmed in by white cliffs, which would not exactly make it easy for animals to be driven along. The water gushes into a grotto which today is quite overgrown. Those who wish to refresh themselves with a cool drink should bring a mug and a piece of string to bring the not particularly tempting liquid into the daylight. It is not the fountain but the scenery which makes the walk worth while.

Perachóri: a walk of approximately 1¾ hours along an asphalted road.

Everybody should spend an evening during a stay on Ithaca on the terrace of the little kafenío in Perachóri. The view of the lights of Vathí is worth the cost of the taxi fare back. But there is also something to do in Perachóri before the sun goes down: a walk to the scanty remains of the medieval capital of the island, *Paleóchora*, 10–15 minutes from Perachóri. The ruins of a former church

dedicated to St John the Evangelist stand here and, although there is no roof, the paintings on the screen can still be clearly made out. They follow the strict Byzantine rules and depict from left to right, as was customary, first the patron of the church, in this case John with the eagle as his symbol, then Mary, Christ and finally John the Baptist. The paintings probably date from the 16th c.

Cave of the Nymphs *(Spíleo tón Nimfón):* the round trip takes about 4–5 hours on foot.

You get to the Cave of the Nymphs (take your torch with you!) by heading out of Vathí in a north-westerly direction and then taking the signposted fork along a field footpath to the cave. At the sign which points to the 'Kassonaki Sculptured Grave', walk 10 m to the right

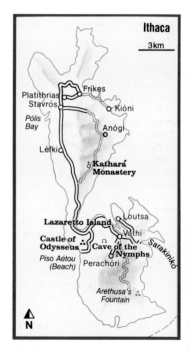

and you will be standing in front of the entrance to the cave in which Odysseus on his return to Ithaca is supposed to have hidden the treasure which he had brought with him. An iron staircase leads down into the little inner chamber where shapes formed by stalactites look, by a stretch of the imagination, like the nymphs referred to by Homer, sitting at their looms. An opening in the roof also fits in with Homer's description: the cave was said to have two entrances, one for mortals and the other for immortals.

After visiting the cave, follow the signposted path a little further and in 15 minutes it will lead you to a concealed sarcophagus hewn out of the rock. You can still vaguely make out an animal relief on it which resembles a lion. From here you can make your way down to Vathí through stands of olive and carob trees.

The north of the island

Shortly after the turning to the Cave of the Nymphs, the road takes you to the *Bay of Dexiá*, which the present-day residents of Ithaca like to think of as the harbour of Phorkys where the sleeping Odysseus, together with his treasures, was beached by the Phaeacians from Corfu.

Some 3½ km beyond the town of Vathí, a road branches off to the left which will lead you to the beginning of a signposted footpath. If you follow this, you will come to the ruins of the *'Castle of Odysseus'*. The walls of this 5th c. acropolis are worth looking at. If you follow the road a little further you will arrive at the shingle beach of *Piso Aétou*.

The main road now passes over the narrowest place on the island, which also provides the most breathtaking landscape on Ithaca. The road runs at a

---

 The Odyssey

Odysseus was the first warrior in European history to be late home. Having taken part in the Trojan War, which historians date about 1200 B.C., he was not permitted by the gods to go back to Ithaca and was compelled to wander around the world for ten years before the Olympians finally relented and made it possible for him to return. Where he actually sailed is disputed by modern researchers: some say only as far as Gibraltar, others that he reached Scotland. Some deny his actual existence and look upon the character as a pure fabrication on Homer's part. Homer probably lived in about 800 B.C. and is thought to have been the author of the 'Odyssey'. This is itself a little uncertain as many classical scholars believe that this epic was the work of at least two poets. There is also some doubt about Homer's other masterpiece, the 'Iliad', which is often thought to be the work of another poet altogether.

The doubts do not end there. Whether the Ithaca of the 'Odyssey' identifies with the present island of Ithaca is also called into question. There are some brief descriptions of the island in the 'Odyssey', yet none of these can be seen to refer unmistakably to Ithaca. Wilhelm Dörpfeld, for example, was of the opinion that Lefkás was the Ithaca referred to by Homer, that at one time its inhabitants were banished and subsequently had the name of Ithaca transferred to their new home.

The truth surrounding the wanderings of Odysseus will always be disputed. What the 'Odyssey' actually gives us, apart from great poetry, is a description of the early Greeks, their mental attitudes and their way of life. Although it is not quite clear whether Homer portrays life at the time of the Trojan War or during his own time, he nevertheless provides us with an insight into the early Greek world. That is why the 'Odyssey' is more than just entertaining holiday reading.

considerable height along the top of a mountain ridge which falls away on both sides into the sea — you can almost imagine you are flying. A little further on the road divides. The poor road heading eastwards is the more interesting. At a height of 556 m on this road stands the *Monastery of Kathará* which is only occupied during the summer months. Visitors are welcome and may even stay overnight if they wish.

    Church festival on August 15th.

The road takes you on through a wonderful landscape with strange rock formations to the little hill township of *Anógi* (18 km north of Vathí). A lovely 16th c. church, dedicated to the Virgin Mary, stands here. Inside are the remains of wall paintings dating from 1670, and also of interest are the ladies' gallery and the distinct subdivision of the church into a large part for the men and a smaller one for the women.

The two roads join again in *Stavrós*.

Stavrós

The second largest place on the island (17 km from Vathí) lies 150 m above the west coast. In a tiny park on the square is a bust of Odysseus which was proudly erected by the people of Stavrós when, in the thirties, excavations at nearby *Pelikáta* provided the proof that a palace must have stood here in the 2nd millennium B.C. which could well have been that of Odysseus — a better site in fact than any in the south of the island. Practically nothing remains today of this palace. Nothing that the layman would recognise remains of Odysseus' city either. However, as excavations have shown, it was situated in the *Bay of Pólis* below Stavrós. Odysseus was worshipped here in a cave as long ago as Homer's time, and in the 3rd c. B.C. games were still held in honour of the hero. It is likely that Homer knew of the Odysseus cult in this area and therefore declared Ithaca to be his home.

Fríkes

This is the first seaside resort on the north-east coast of the island (23 km from Vathí). Fishing boats bob up and down in the tiny harbour and it will not take you very long to count the houses in the town. This is the sort of place to spend your holiday if you are looking for as much peace and quiet as possible rather than a good stretch of beach.

      High-standard pottery available.

Kióni

Without a doubt this is the most romantic place on the island (27 km from Vathí). The red-roofed houses climb up the slopes overlooking two small coves and nestle amongst the foliage of the trees and the beautiful floral displays in their well tended gardens. You can sit and dream in the kafenía and tavernas along the peaceful quayside below. If you wish to bathe there are small shingle beaches 10–20 minutes' walk away.

    Pedal boats.

    Boat connections with Vathí twice daily during the summer months.

If you return to Vathí by land, you can take the western road from Stavrós which runs high above the coast. *Léfki* is the only hamlet you will pass through on this road. From here there is a good view over the neighbouring island of Cefalonia and the Daskalió islet. This little island causes the present inhabitants of Ithaca much distress; it is an irritant to all those who want to believe that Ithaca was the home of Odysseus. If it was, then Daskalió must be the Homeric island of Astéris where the suitors of Penelope, the wife of Odysseus, lay in wait for her son Telemachos. Daskalió, however, is very unconvincing as a candidate for Astéris, and doubts remain as to the true home of the hero.

Cefalonia

Cefalonia (Kefallinía)

Cefalonia is not only the largest of the Ionian islands but it is also the least densely populated. The scenery on the island is very varied with deeply indented bays and towering mountain ranges which combine to produce a rich and colourful mosaic. Some parts are fertile and support the inhabitants, but in other parts the soil is poor and capable of growing little more than thyme, oregano, aniseed, rosemary, bay and sage, forcing the population to look for a living as sailors, traders or academics. More university professors have been born on Cefalonia, according to the local people, than on any of the other islands.

Foreign tourism is concentrated mainly in the immediate vicinity of the capital Argostóli which, like all other places on the island, has been almost completely rebuilt following the severe earthquake of 1953. This earthquake signalled the end of one of the mysterious natural phenomena for which Cefalonia is well known. Two massive chunks of rock rose from the sea off the southern tip of the Palikí Peninsula and until 1953 they moved constantly towards and away from each other. This movement was not apparent to the naked eye but it was clearly noticeable if, for example, a stick was clamped between the two rocks. It is said that the captain of a British ship tried to pull one of the rocks away from the other by attaching a rope to it. When the line was untied, the rock promptly returned to its partner…

There are still many natural wonders on Cefalonia, including some mysterious ones which remain unexplained to this day. The island is also blessed with good beaches. Even if you plan to spend several weeks here you are unlikely to get bored as there are so many interesting places to visit. For these reasons alone, Cefalonia's future as a tourist centre can only be rosy.

Argostóli Pop. 7200

The capital of the island lies on a bay with no view of the open sea, giving the feeling of being on a large inland lake. On the other side of the water the island is mountainous, some of the peaks being over 1000 m high and providing a majestic background for the lively activity in the town. This activity is not to be found along the esplanade, however, but rather on *Lithóstratos Street*, the principal thoroughfare, and on the *Platía Valiános* which adjoins the street's northern end. Lithóstratos means 'stone', and the street is so named because it was formerly the only paved street in the town. Almost everyone in Argostóli, residents and visitors alike, can be seen on the huge wide Platía Valiános at least once during the evening. Hundreds of tables and chairs entice you to have something to eat and drink, while hordes of children play football, their favourite game, among the crowds of people.

There are two museums in Argostóli which are worth seeing, but one especially deserves a visit: the *Laografikó Mousío* (Folklore Museum) which is housed in the Korialénios Library.

Numerous photographs from the period before and immediately after the earthquake show clearly how beautiful the old Argostóli was, and just how much devastation was caused in 1953. In addition, you can see a large number of old icons, examples of embroidery and weaving, and other memorabilia which recall an earlier way of life.

The *Archaeological Museum* (100 m from the Folklore Museum on Lithóstratos Street) contains, in three separate rooms, mainly discoveries from the Mycenaean period, but also archaic and classical vases, Hellenistic gold jewellery and Roman glassware.

 La Gondola, Italian-Greek garden restaurant on the Platía Valiános which has a high standard of service but is rather expensive.

 Makrís Yalós and *Platís Yalós*. Lovely, well maintained sandy beaches approximately 3–4 km from the town. Bus service.

Makrís Yalós:

 Pedal boats and canoes.

Diving school at the *Hotel Méditerranée*.

S At the *Hotel Méditerranée*.

Platís Yalós:

 Pedal boats.

 Sweets and roasted nuts produced in Cefalonia are available from confectioners' shops on the Platía Valiános.

 Moped and scooter hire.

Several times daily to Lixoúri.

🚌 Excursions from Argostóli

Yíro tis Lássis

The northern tip of the Lássis Peninsula on which Argostóli stands is circuited by an 8-km-long road. If you head north out of the town along the coast, you will soon come to a restaurant, next to which a huge paddle wheel will attract your

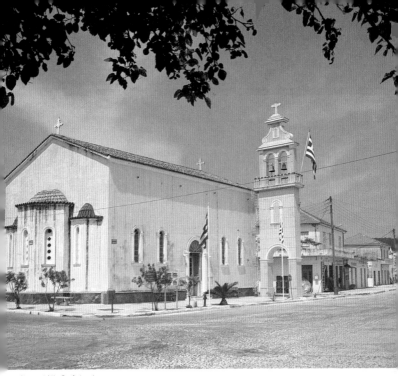

Argostóli, Cefalonia

attention. It is the only surviving, and restored, part of one of the famous seawater mills of Cefalonia. On this stretch of the coast the seawater flows inland through a series of narrow channels, many of which were at one time subterranean, and seeps away into the surrounding karst hills. To experts on the subject these underground channels are known as *katavothra*. When an Englishman discovered this natural wonder in 1835, he immediately put it to good use and ran a corn mill, using the water which flowed in from the sea. Others had similar ideas and in 1926 one of these sea mills was adapted to provide the islanders and the tourists with a supply of ice for their cold drinks. But the 1953 earthquake brought this cheap source of energy to an end.

The water which trickles away here reappears, above sea level, about 16 km away. Now everybody knows that water cannot flow uphill but on Cefalonia it seems to be possible. How can this be? Scientists are not of one mind on the matter but the most obvious explanation seems to be that somewhere along the way fresh water from springs at a higher level flows into the underground tunnels, producing the pressure which causes the water to rise above sea level. The mystery of *where* the water seeping away close to Argostóli reappears was solved at the beginning of the sixties; a team of geographers from the university of Graz poured yellow dye into the water at the sea mill near Argostóli and it came up again in the cave of Melissáni (see page 74).

The other interesting sight on this short circular route is a lighthouse which looks more like a classical temple, *Ágios Theodóros*. The rotunda was built in Doric style by the British in 1820. It was destroyed in 1953 and subsequently rebuilt in a simplified form.

Circular tour through the Livathó region (20–30 km)

Roughly twenty-five villages are scattered around this region, which is the most fertile on the island. Grapes and olives are the most important crops. Only half a day is really needed to get to know the area.

The journey from Argostóli takes you first above the beach and hotels of Makrís Yalós. A short way beyond the approach to the Hotel Méditerranée a road leads off to the left and winds upwards to the tiny *Monastery of Ágios Yerásimos*. St Yerásimos (often written Gerásimos) is the patron saint of the island. He came from the Peloponnese, lived on Cefalonia during the 16th c., fought against the Venetians for the preservation of the Orthodox faith and was canonised after his death. Credit is given to him even today for miracles which he is supposed to have performed during his lifetime. He lived for some time on this site, in a cave in front of which the present monastery was built at a later date. When the only remaining monk is present, it is possible to look around the building.

The main road continues alongside the beach of Platís Yalós and once past the airport it goes on to Kourkoumeláta.

Kourkoumeláta was completely destroyed in the 1953 earthquake. Fortunately, however, a shipowner by the name of Veryótis, who was a native of the town and had made a lot of money, donated some of his wealth to the rebuilding of all the houses. This represented a show of loyalty typical of

the Greeks. As soon as a Greek becomes a millionaire he endows ˉa museum, a monument or a school to the town of his birth, even though he might have long since lived in Athens, New York or Hollywood.

Metaxáta. This town, which is probably the greenest on the island and is rich in gardens full of flowers, was for some months in 1823 the home of the poet Lord Byron. The affluence of Metaxáta is obvious. Shipowners and businessmen raised on the island spend their holidays here and there is little room for the tourist. It is best to admire the town and just drive on.

You will be amazed by the Mycenaean necropolis which is signposted from the main road. *Táfi Mazarakáton* is written on the sign. Here you can see better than anywhere else in Greece how the nobility were buried about 3200 years ago. There is something fascinating about the loneliness of the area which you may walk around even though it is enclosed. Typical of the tombs of that period is the *drómos*, a shaft which gives access to the actual burial chamber in which several corpses were buried in niches hewn out of the rock.

A short distance further on, a signposted road on the other side branches off to the *convent of Ágios Andréas*. The nuns show visitors around the 18th c. convent church and they also have the key to an older church, a little off the beaten track, which was built in the 17th c. and houses a series of impressive wall paintings. The next place you come to is *Travliáta* which almost immediately merges into the neighbouring village of *Peratáta*. The huge walls of the Byzantine fortress *Ágios Geórgios* are clearly visible above both villages and may be reached by car or on foot. In Venetian times these walls surrounded the medieval island capital, in places to a height of 25 m. In those days everybody readily retreated into the

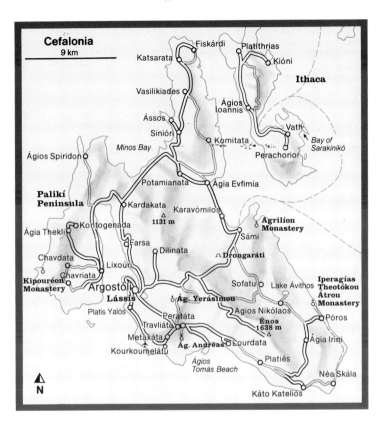

interior of the island to seek cover from raids, although the harbour which was their lifeline (the bay of Argostóli) lay several miles away. It was not until after this harbour silted up in the 17th c. that the residents moved back to the present-day Argostóli; they pronounced it the capital of the island in 1765.

On the way back to Argostóli at the place where the road meets the coast, enthusiastic amateur archaeologists can set out on a game of 'hunt the ruins'. Lying scattered around this area are scanty remains of the ancient city of *Kráne* which was the largest of the four towns on the island more than 2000

years ago.

The convent of Ágios Yerásimos
(about 15 km).

The most famous convent on the island is also the least attractive to the tourist because the old convent building, founded by the island's patron saint in 1570, was totally destroyed by the earthquake in 1953 and later replaced by thoroughly uninteresting new buildings. The plane tree in the courtyard is said to be all that remains from the year in which the convent was originally built. If the tiny convent chapel is unlocked, you can see the highly honoured mummified remains of the saint, which are carried around in a glass-fronted processional palanquin on his feast days.

    August 16th and October 20th.

Circular tour through the southern part of the island
(about 100 km)

From Argostóli the route first takes you past the old island capital of *Ágios Geórgios* and through the twin towns of Travliáta and Peratáta. By taking a short detour off the main road you will come to the idyllic little beach of *Ágios Tomás*.

    Galini: you can always enjoy fresh fish here, on a terrace overlooking the sea with a magnificent roof of grape vines as your cover. Cod in garlic sauce is particularly recommended (bakalyáros me skordaliá).

You drive on through villages full of flowers, past isolated palm trees and splendid araucarias, olive groves and cypresses, until you reach Platiés. You leave the main road here and turn off towards the coast to *Káto Kateliós* which is still quite an unspoilt fishing village, with several tavernas by the beach.

Néa Skála is the next place on the coast, and here art-lovers will be in their element. Within the ruins of a Roman villa two 2nd c. mosaics have been preserved, one of which depicts the *trittía*, a sacrifice of three animals to three different gods, and the other an allegory of envy: a young man is being torn apart by wild animals, as if by his own envy. In addition there is a long shady beach at Néa Skála.

     Pedal boats.

A little further on, the coastal road becomes nothing more than a rough track. A short distance beyond Néa

Skála a small church, *Ágios Geórgios*, stands on the right-hand side of the road. About twelve blocks of stone and six sections of columns, whitewashed in places, part of an ancient temple dating from the 6th c. B.C., were used in the building of this church. The foundations of the temple can be made out 15 m away.

Póros is one of the Cefalonian coastal resorts which is often frequented by Greeks during the holiday season. The beach is a long one but is almost without any shade. The scenery which provides

Sámi, Cefalonia

the background is very much more attractive than the core of buildings put up by the modern-day Greeks.

  Pedal boats, canoes.

 Killíni, Peloponnese.

On the return journey from Póros you will go through a short but impressive ravine. About 1½ km beyond Póros a track, signposted to the *Iperagías Theotókou Átrou Monastery*, branches off to the right but suddenly comes to an end after 1.7 km. If you climb uphill from here for about an hour on a marked path you will come to the enormous monastery tower which was originally only accessible by means of a rope ladder.

Ágios Nikólaos is the next point you reach on this magnificent scenic route. At the village a signposted path branches off to *Lake Ávithos*. This reed-fringed pool, with a diameter of no more than 10–15 m, irrigates the whole of this fertile valley down to Póros. The pool is supposed to be so deep that not even a modern echo-sounder can penetrate to the bottom.

The climb now proceeds steadily upwards to the slopes of the highest mountain in the Ionian islands, *Mount Énos* (1628 m). From here you not only have a spectacular view but you can also see a unique pine forest which is made up of a particularly dark species of pine indigenous to the island. The botanical name of these trees is *abies cephalonica*. You can wander around at will up here. It is about 25 km back to Argostóli.

Sámi Pop. approx. 1000

This typical little Greek port is really only brought to life by the incoming and outgoing passengers. Historically, the town has only experienced one glorious evening: the eve of the naval battle of Lepanto fought in the year 1571, when the western fleet under the command of Don Juan of Austria, half-brother of the Spanish King Philip II, gathered here. The following day they annihilated the Turkish fleet and so ensured the ascendancy of Spain and of the other western countries in the Mediterranean for some years.

 Patras, Ithaca, Paxos, Corfu, Igoumenítsa and Brindisi.

 Environs of Sámi

Old Sámi

A romantic half day's walk takes you up into the hills which lie directly behind Sámi, where the remains of the ancient city can still be seen.

First follow the path leading to the *Agrilíon Monastery* for a little way. When you come to a sign pointing right towards the monastery, turn uphill and keep straight on. A hill with the clearly visible remains of the ancient city walls rises up on the right-hand edge of a plateau. After crossing this plain you will come across a farmstead, behind which the remains of ancient walls and foundations blend in beautifully with the old ruined monastery. The solitude up here and the view looking down on to Sámi harbour, which seems so close, the coastline and the sea will surely make the walk unforgettable.

The cave of Drongaráti (roughly 4 km in the direction of Argostóli). Stone steps lead down into a cavern full of stalactites. In 1977 the famous Greek composer Míkis Theodorákis held a concert in the cavern, which is approximately 200 m in diameter.

Karavómilos and the cave of Melissáni (approx. 4 km)

Below the village of Karavómilos a small lake lies close to the seashore. It is fed by a spring which is linked by way of the cave of Melissáni with the sea mills of Argostóli. A water mill also operated here years ago. The main attraction of the sea-shore today is a taverna set under tall eucalyptus trees where many peaceful hours may be spent admiring the view over Sámi and the sea. There is even a pedal boat on the lake which you could hire for a voyage of discovery through the man-high reeds. The cave of *Melissáni* is only a kilometre away but it is very much higher up the hillside. The seawater which seeps underground near Argostóli sees the light of day again, almost 48 hours later, at this point.

The cave is open to tourists and boat trips are available on the lake which practically fills its whole area. The first part of the cave is open to the daylight owing to a roof collapse brought about by various earthquakes; the remains now lie in the centre of the lake which is in many places over 20 m deep. The bottom can be quite clearly seen through the crystal-clear water. Trees cling to the rim above and roots creep downwards over the rocks, creating a strange and atmospheric picture. The

Fiskárdi

second part of the cave is, as caves should be, completely roofed over, but here it is the stalagmites and the shapes formed by them which look like roots. In places they are completely overgrown with moss, moulding the ground into little trees and bushes, reminding you of Bonsai trees.

The northern and western parts of Cefalonia

The northern tip of Cefalonia, largely barren and producing very little, runs almost parallel to the neighbouring island of Ithaca. As you travel from the south the first stop worth making is at the village of *Sinióri*. You can get refreshments here before starting out on the rough, precipitous side road, full of twists and turns, which will take you down to the *Bay of Mírtos*. This is a long stretch of beach, of sand and pebbles, over 100 m wide in most places and set in front of a steeply rising coastline. Apart from a few campers hardly anyone ever finds his way here and you can have the beach almost entirely to yourself.

Ássos

If you are looking for peace and tranquillity then this small, quiet seaside resort, lying on a spit of land at the end of a whole series of tiny, fairly inaccessible coves, can be well recommended. The sharply rising coastline in the background makes an impressive scene. The steep slopes of a peninsula crowned by a massive Venetian fortress (*Frourion*) rise up opposite the dreamy fishing harbour with its few tavernas. The mighty walls of the fortress have been almost taken over by the lush vegetation growing wild within its protective boundaries. The fortress was built during the late 16th c.

Fiskárdi

This town was formerly known as Panórmo and is very much more lively than Ássos. During the summer months boats carrying holidaymakers from Lefkás and Ithaca arrive here at least once a day, and yachts are a common sight. The 1953 earthquake caused relatively little damage, so the character of the town has remained much the same through the years.

In addition to its perfect setting the village has another attraction which will be of interest to those who have an appreciation of history. On the northern side of the harbour are the ruins of a church with the stumps of two towers flanking the west front. The church was probably built in the 11th c. when the Normans plied the seas around Greece. One of their most famous leaders was the cruel but successful Robert Guiscard who died on July 17th 1085 in the village which since that time has borne the name of Fiskárdi — an approximate version of his name. The church was probably built in his honour at that time, perhaps even to house temporarily his mortal remains.

A Special Tip

Holidaymakers can stay in Fiskárdi in villas formerly owned by the aristocracy. The Greek Tourist Office has had them restored and decorated in traditional style. Ask your local travel agent for further details.

Lixoúri Pop. 2850

Lixoúri, the third largest town on the island after Argostóli and Sámi, is situated in the western part of Cefalonia on the Palikí Peninsula. There is really little of interest here, although a short trip by taxi or car to the *Monastery of Kipouréon* could be rewarding. The monastery was founded in 1759 on the western slopes of the peninsula and has in its custody some precious icons and other valuable church treasures. It is possible to spend the night here.

Zákinthos

Zákinthos

The Venetians gave this island off the west coast of the Peloponnese the shortened name of Zante, and also referred to it by the affectionate name of *Fior di Levante* (Flower of the East). Even today Italians feel particularly content and at home on Zákinthos.

The island capital of the same name, with its campanile which towers up to the sky, has an Italian air about it, and the flat, delightful, well wooded landscape reminds you, even more than does Corfu, of similar scenery in the north of the Apennine peninsula. Yet the islanders have remained true Greeks. During the period of the Venetian occupation (1482–1797) they constantly rebelled against their uninvited foreign rulers. In the first half of the last century, and against the wishes of the British, they supported the freedom fighters on the Greek mainland in their struggle against the Turks, as did the inhabitants of the other Ionian islands.

As a holiday island, Zákinthos is visited mainly by Italians and Greeks, who prefer to spend their vacation in the capital. Germans and Austrians usually stay in the seaside resort of Laganás and the British go to Argássi. There are numerous good beaches and organised excursions. Those who wish to explore on their own, however, will soon discover that there are far fewer signposts here than on the other islands.

Spring on Zákinthos

Zákinthos town Pop. 10,000

The capital of the island extends a good 2 km along the water's edge against a backdrop of white rock and green trees. The heart of the town is formed by the Platía Solomoú on the sea front and the smaller, more intimate Platía Ágiou Márkou a little further inland.

Two monuments were erected on the *Solomós Square* to commemorate two great Greek poets of the last century, both of whom were born on Zákinthos: Ugo Fóscolo (1778) and Dionísios Solomós (1798). Fóscolo, the son of a Venetian and a Greek, later went to Italy and wrote works in Italian which promoted the freedom and unification of Italy. Solomós did the same for Greece. Among other things he wrote the words of the Greek national anthem.

Also in Solomós Square is the *Church of Ágios Nikólaos* which is worth seeing. After the earthquake it was painstakingly restored, and it contains a splendidly carved wooden screen. But the square is dominated by the arcaded façade of the two-storeyed *museum* which has on display in its numerous rooms icons, frescos and paintings by masters of the so-called Ionian School. These were Greek artists of the 18th and early 19th c.

who based their work mainly on western models but rarely departed from their provincial style.

There is a second museum on *Ágios Márkos Square*, a place of pilgrimage in fact for the Greeks, the *Solomós Museum*. In a mausoleum on the ground floor the poet Solomós and his colleague Andréas Kálvos (born in Zákinthos in 1792) lie buried. In the remaining rooms there are mementos of Solomós, as well as icons, paintings, 18th c. costumes and many other items of interest. The episcopal church of *St Mark*, which serves the Roman Catholic population, stands next to the museum but is unfortunately kept locked most of the time.

With its tall campanile, the *Church of St Dionísios* at the southern end of the town is the principal landmark. The remains of the island's patron saint are preserved here and like those of St Spiridon on Corfu are carried through the town twice a year in a ceremonial procession. Modern wall paintings in the traditional style decorate the interior of the church, which is well worth seeing.

Mallias, a large garden restaurant in the Platía Ágiou Márkou, has an unusually wide choice of dishes. Particularly recommended: stifádo (beef with onions), fish soup, swordfish and lamprey with garlic sauce (galéo skordaliá).

Well maintained toll-beach run by the Greek Tourist Office (EOT) just a few metres to the north of Solomós Square.

Ágios Charalámbos.

Mopeds and motor scooters.

Processions in honour of St Dionísios on August 24th and December 17th.

Right: Zákinthos

Connections several times daily with Killíni in the Peloponnese.

 ## Bochális and the Venetian fortress

There is an interesting walk up the rocky hill behind the town which leads to this medieval fortress. On the way there you may like to make a short detour to the small, unpretentious little chapel of *Ágios Geórgios* where, at the beginning of the Greek War of Independence in 1821, local patriots formed a 'society of friends' (*Filikí Etería*) which supported with weapons and money the men fighting on the Peloponnese.

From the village of Bochális there is a magnificent view over the town and the sea. It is just a few steps from here to the extensive fortress which is interesting not only because of its well preserved walls but also for the small area of sub-tropical woodland which has grown up within its fortifications.

 Mona Liza, taverna with a splendid panoramic view.

To Kastro taverna; *kantades,* typical Zákinthos songs, are sung here every evening.

On the return journey you could make a detour into the narrow river valley at the side of the road, where among the houses you will come across a *cemetery* with monumental grave stones. This is the last resting place of many Britons who died on Zákinthos during the period of the British Protectorate.

The south-east of the island

Dominated by *Mount Skopós* (492 m) this peninsula which bears the same name is truly idyllic with its pine forests, sheer cliffs and beautiful coves.

Argássi is scarcely more than a village built along a single street. It has a small stretch of beach, some hotels and a Venetian bridge which is no longer usable and now stands in the shallows

just offshore. The road then snakes uphill to some splendid viewpoints and several good, sandy bays.

 Ágios Nikólaos Beach.   Pedal boats.

 Mavrantzis Beach.   Windsurfing school.

 Porta Roma, a tiny bay set between white cliffs.

 Gerakas Beach (mainly naturist).   Canoes.

Laganás (8 km from Zákinthos town)

An 8-km-long broad sandy beach extends the entire length of the shoreline of the Bay of Laganás, which is framed by the Skopós and Kerí peninsulas. The town is quite built up and has many hotels and guest houses. In summer it becomes very crowded and cars are even driven about on the sand, which does not exactly please every visitor.

A Special Tip

The beach of Laganás and the sandy beaches in the northern part of the bay are some of the last remaining places where reticulated turtles, a threatened species, lay their eggs. Greedy locals and inquisitive visitors have been responsible for reducing from 1300 to about 700 the number of turtles which come ashore here every year. Everyone can help to protect this reptile. Do not go on to these beaches at night, and resist any offer from local people to show you where the turtles lay their eggs. Make it abundantly clear that the continued existence of this species is more important to you than a photograph!

Laganás beach

Limín Keríou and Kerí (20 km from Zákinthos town)

When you drive southwards out of Laganás it is worth breaking your journey at the *Bay of Limín Keríou*. Nowadays it is just a tiny harbour with a few houses and a rather poor stony beach. In ancient times, however, it was an extremely well known town, even mentioned by Herodotos. It was pitch which made the fortune of the people of Kerí in those days. Some few hundred metres inland in a region full of swamps and marshes there are several ponds and pools from which the people were once able to extract pitch with the aid of myrtle branches. Pitch was used throughout Greece, mainly in shipbuilding. You can still discover these pitch lakes and, if you wish, extract your own personal sample of pitch. There is not enough of it today, however, for it to be a commercial proposition.

Rabbit and goat meat, and on occasions lobster, are particular specialities available from the two tavernas in Limín Keríou.

Kerí is a small hill village which lies at the end of the road. Although the going is rough, you can take quiet walks from here over the Kerí peninsula, for example to the lighthouse on *Cape Marathía.*

Circular tour through the mid-eastern part of the island (about 45 km)

Olive trees and vines grown for both wine and currants will accompany you throughout this pleasant trip; olive branches even hang over and on to the narrow roads. The industrious people of Zákinthos also plant crops beneath the olive trees. From now on the countryside is for the most part flat, and it is thus all the more surprising when lovely views suddenly appear before you from the slight hills which you do encounter. In the villages chickens and geese, goats

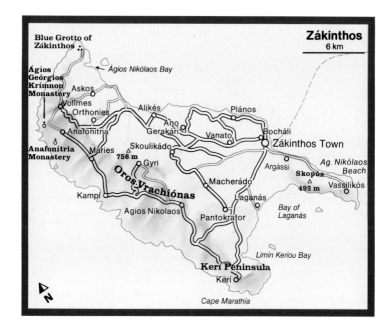

and donkeys are as entitled as you to the use of the road — so please take care.

Plános is a small village lying just beyond the coastal resort of Tsiliví with its long beach of fine sand.

  In Tsiliví.

  Pedal boats.

Áno Gerakári is a still unspoilt little village situated on the slopes of a hill, on top of which stands the *Church of St Nicholas* with its modern concrete bell-tower. From up here there is a splendid view over the green plain far below with its tall, straight cypress trees, and over the mountains of the Óros Vrachiónas range which rise up almost abruptly behind it, and which reach a height of 756 m.

Alikés is the fourth seaside resort on the island. Translated its name means 'saltpans', and these still occupy a large area between the sea and the mountains. The salt is usually collected in September. A few fishing boats are moored at the pier at Alikés but otherwise, during the summer months, the people make a living mainly from the holidaymakers. Immediately you enter the town, you will encounter a strange relic from the past. Astride the stream on the right-hand side of the road is an old Venetian arched bridge which you can still walk across.

  A long, gently shelving beach of fine sand which is particularly safe for children.

  Pedal boats, canoes.

  Cycles and mopeds.

Skoulikádo, like many other villages in this fertile region, nestles close to the mountain range which borders it to the west, making maximum use of the arable land available. The bell-tower of the village church is particularly large.

Macherádo is a place of pilgrimage for many islanders who visit the *Church of Ágia Mávra* to worship the miracle-working icon of St Mávra. Grateful believers have given her a silver-gilt casing as well as precious stones and jewels. A necklace which belonged to Olga, formerly Queen of Greece, adorns the icon which dates from the period around 1600. The richly carved screen is a work of the 18th c. although the church itself was built a century later. The overall picture in the interior, with its combination of western paintings and Byzantine icons, represents a rather unfortunate attempt to blend two different artistic concepts.

  St Mávra's Day on the first Sunday in June.

The north-west of the island

(round trip of about 90 km from Zákinthos town)

The road begins to climb steeply behind Alikés and the vegetation changes completely, giving way to a covering of scrub. The scenery changes once again when you reach the high plateau, where cornfields predominate, while a little further on you will suddenly come upon a copse resounding with a loud chorus of cicadas. Here in the north-west the character of Zákinthos is totally different from that in the southern part of the island.

Anafonítria is the base for a short trip to the *Monastery of Anafonítria* which is no longer inhabited but which is still kept open for visitors and is consequently well maintained. The enormous fortified tower at the entrance testifies to the age of the monastery. It was founded in the early 15th c. at the time when Zákinthos,

together with the other Ionian islands, including Corfu and Paxos, was still under the rule of the Italian Tocco family. An old oven and an olive press may still be seen inside the tower. The monastery church contains 17th c. wall paintings which are difficult to discern, but the several icons which have been mounted with gold or silver are of interest. Special attention is paid to the monastery by the local people as it was here that, in the role of abbot, the patron saint of the island, Dionísios, spent the last years of his life. He even sheltered the murderer of his own brother in the monastery to protect him from prosecution, a remarkable deed which has always earned him enormous respect in the eyes of the people.

A signposted track leading out of Anafonítria will take you to the *Monastery of Ágios Geórgios Krímnon*. This monastery, surrounded by walls and set in dense woodland, is inhabited by just one monk who will always receive visitors, except during the middle of the day. The monastery which was founded in the 16th c. has its own, quite large, visitors' wing, which is evidence of its former importance, as is the massive fortified tower, now in ruins. The meeting with the monk, the peace and the solitude constitute the particular charm of this monastery. The church, however, with its Baroque decoration, seems totally out of place. By the way, the monk is not only grateful for donations of money but he is also pleased to receive any provisions you may be able to bring him!

Leaving the monastery you can drive further along the track to the village of Volímes and from there on a tarred road down to the *Blue Grotto of Zákinthos*. There are in fact at least three grottos, which can be reached by boat from the *Bay of Ágios Nikólaos*. The master of the boat usually allows time for a swim in the cool waters of the caverns where the lighting effects are extremely good.

Kýthira and Antikýthira (Kíthira and Andikíthira)

Note: Since the general opinion is against including these islands in the Ionian chain, and as it is extremely difficult to get to Kýthira from the other Ionian islands, they are only briefly commented on here.

Politically, the two islands which lie between the Peloponnese and Crete come under the administrative district (*nómos*) of Attica, which consists mainly of Athens and the Attic Peninsula. Geographically, the islands belong to the southern Aegean archipelago which stretches from the Peloponnese via Kýthira and Antikýthira, Crete, Kassos, Karpathos and Rhodes to the Asia Minor coast of Turkey. Economically, the two islands are linked to the Peloponnese and Australia; the Peloponnese because they are right next to it, and Australia because that is where many of the former inhabitants live today. History forms the only possible link between Kýthira and Antikýthira and the Ionian islands, and even then only during the period when they came under foreign rule. In this respect, they formed a unity with the Ionian islands from 1797 to 1864. To begin with they were ruled by the French, then by the Russians, then again by the French and finally by the British, up to the time of union with Greece. Even during the period when the islands from Corfu to Zákinthos were occupied by the Venetians or the Turks, the two islands of Kýthira went their own way. Until 1363 Kýthira was directly governed by the Venieri family who were of aristocratic Venetian blood, and Antikýthira was administered by the Viaro family until 1797 and then by the Foscarini and Giustiniani families.

Kýthira

The historical capital of the island is *Chóra* which is also called Kýthira like the island itself. The village, which will remind you of the Cyclades with its flat-roofed houses, lies almost 300 m above sea level and is dominated by the ruins of a Venetian fortress. It overlooks the little harbour of *Kapsali* which is worth a visit. The ships from Piraeus and the Peloponnese tie up at *Ágia Pelágia*, where there are two lovely sandy beaches and the sea is very inviting.

The picturesque village of *Milopótamos,* and *Pótamos,* the largest place on the island, are both worth visiting. Nothing remains today of the ancient Greek shrine of Aphrodite near Paleóchora.

✈ During the summer months, flight connections in small propeller-driven aircraft can be made once or twice daily to Athens.

🚢 Connections up to three times weekly with Piraeus, and with Kastelli in Crete. Also with Neapolis, Gythion and Monemvassia on the Peloponnese. Hovercraft operate four times a week from Zea Marina/Piraeus.

Antikýthira

This almost treeless island is inhabited by a little over one hundred people. Tourists are not catered for here and there are no hotels — making it an ideal spot for those holidaymakers in search of solitude.

Kýthira

Kýthira

Useful things to know

Before you go

Climate

The Ionian islands are no place for a winter holiday. The tourist season begins at the end of March and ends in October. The average daytime temperatures usually exceed 20°C from May onwards, rising in July and August to 31° or 32°C. The average night-time temperature never exceeds 18°. Although most rain falls during the winter it occasionally rains in summer too and only the months of June, July and August have little or no rain.

It is possible to bathe in the sea between the middle of May and October. The water temperature rises from 18°C in May to 24°C in August, and then drops to 18° again in October.

What to take

Depending on the time of your holiday you should take clothing suitable for the temperatures given above. Sunglasses are a necessity and an insect repellent is essential during the hottest months. Stout footwear is recommended for those who intend to do much walking, as many minor roads are somewhat rough. In the larger resorts most items required on holiday are obtainable. Films, however, are very expensive in Greece and visitors are recommended to take an adequate supply.

First-aid kit. Although many preparations can be obtained in Greece (see Chemists, page 87) you would be well advised to have your own simple first-aid kit with you. You should be sure to take any medicines which have been prescribed for you or which you regularly use at home.

Insurance

Although as EC citizens British visitors are entitled to medical treatment equivalent to that provided for the Greeks, nevertheless it is advisable to take out private health insurance for the duration of the holiday, including cover for a flight home in an emergency. To obtain benefit under EC agreements it is essential for a UK national to be in possession of form E 111 obtainable from the Department of Health and Social Security; an application form is available from DHSS offices or main post offices.

Accommodation

Most visitors book package tours which include hotels, etc., but if you are travelling independently details of accommodation can be obtained from the *Greek National Tourist Organisation* in London (see page 91).

Getting to Corfu

By air: British Airways and Olympic Airways operate several flights a week from London. There are also many charter flights from Great Britain, especially in the summer. Services from Athens operate throughout the year to Corfu, Lefkás, Cefalonia and Zákinthos.

By sea: Ferries run throughout the year to Corfu from Italy (Venice, Ancona and Brindisi) and from June to September from Brindisi to Cefalonia. During the summer there are services to Corfu from Otranto, Bari, Split, Rijeka, Dubrovnik and Bar. Most of the ships carry cars. There are no services between Piraeus and the Ionian islands.

Immigration and Customs

Passports: Holders of valid British passports can visit Greece for up to three months without a visa.

Vehicle documents: To take a car into Greece a British driving licence is necessary (nationals of the Republic of Ireland need an international driving licence). In addition, the car registration document, nationality plate or sticker and insurance cover are compulsory. The 'green card' is no longer obligatory within the EC but full comprehensive cover is advisable.

Entry: Personal effects required during the holiday and gifts of limited value may be taken into the country duty-free. Equipment of a high value, such as expensive sports equipment, must be recorded in the owner's passport in order to ensure re-export from the islands.

Unlimited amounts of foreign currency can be imported but amounts exceeding the equivalent· of 1000 US dollars should be declared. Only up to 200,000 drachmas can be taken in.

The usual duty-free allowances common in the EC apply to Greece; if purchased in an EC country these are 300 cigarettes or 150 cigarillos or 75 cigars or 400 grammes tobacco, 5 litres wine and 1½ litres spirits over 22% proof. If purchased on an aircraft or in a duty-free shop these amounts are reduced by approximately one third. These concessions apply only to those who are 17 years of age and over.

Exit: A limit of 25,000 drachmas may be taken out of the country and currency up to the equivalent of 1000 US dollars can be exported only if this has been declared on entry.

The duty-free allowances on re-entry into Great Britain are the same as those stated above.

During your stay
Archaeological sites and museums
All the archaeological sites on the Ionian islands are always open and viewing is free of charge. The tourist offices and hotels will provide information about the opening times of museums. On production of an International Student Card students may obtain a reduction in entrance fees to museums, and artists with a UNESCO pass, professors and students of Classics with a certificate from their university or from the Greek Ministry of Culture, and journalists with an International Press Pass have free entry anywhere.

Camping
Camping on unauthorised sites in Greece is forbidden and is a punishable offence. There are eleven camping sites on Corfu, five sites on Lefkás and two on Cefalonia.

Chemists
Chemists' shops (ΦAPMAKEION — Farmakíon) are recognisable by a red Maltese Cross on a white background. In Greece many more pharmaceutical items may be purchased without prescription than in Great Britain and a large number of Greek, Anglo-American and French treatments are sold. Mild painkillers are obtainable from any kiosk. Opening times: Monday, Wednesday and Saturday 8.30 a.m.–2.30 p.m.; Tuesday, Thursday and Friday 8.30 a.m.–1.30 p.m. and 5–8 p.m.

Currency
The unit of Greek currency is the drachma, divided into 100 lepta which no longer play a significant role in everyday life. The rate of exchange fluctuates daily and is the same at all banks. In Great Britain the exchange rates are published in the national newspapers. Usually a better rate is obtainable in Greece than in the UK. As banks at the airports and seaports are

not always open, it is recommended that tourists take a basic amount of Greek currency with them. All Greek banks and post offices change currency, travellers' cheques and Eurocheques. The latter are issued in Greek currency, the highest amount being 25,000 drachmas per cheque. Banks are open from Monday to Friday 8 a.m.–2 p.m.; in tourist resorts they are often also open in the afternoon. Withdrawals from post office savings books are not possible in Greece. Credit cards are accepted on all the islands.

Diving

In order to protect the numerous cultural treasures still lying buried under the sea, diving with breathing apparatus is normally forbidden in Greece. There are a few exceptions, however, for the Ionian islands.

Corfu: Diving with breathing apparatus is allowed between Cape Róda and Cape Drastis within an area of 500 m from the shore. The same applies along the coast from Paleokastrítsa to Cape Arkoudoula (apart from the area around the Lagoúdia islands), as well as along the coast from Cape Kountouri to Cape Agni, apart from the area around the islands of Vidos and Lazaretto.

Cefalonia: Diving with breathing apparatus is permitted within a 500-m-wide stretch along the whole of the coast, with these exceptions: between Fiskárdi and Antisámi Bay, between Cape Capri and Cape Munta, between Cape Ortholithia and Cape Atheras, between the Bay of Sámi and Ágia Efimía, in the Bay of Sámi itself and in the area around the Atheras peninsula.

Zákinthos: Diving with breathing apparatus is permitted within a 500-m-wide stretch along the entire coast.

Should any antiquities be discovered in these waters they must neither be touched nor photographed and the police must be informed immediately.

Electricity

The standard voltage is 220, 50 cycles A.C. On board ship it is usually 110 volts. Sockets are either 2- or 3-pin and plug adaptors are available.

Health

It is probably better for a foreigner to pay any doctor's fees in cash. Ask for a receipt and claim a refund on your return home (see Insurance). In an emergency, to contact a doctor ask the hotel reception, a taxi driver or the landlord of a kafeníon. Otherwise you should adhere to the doctor's consultation times, which are usually 8–11 a.m. and 5–7 p.m.

Hotels and other accommodation

Greek hotels are divided into six categories — L (luxury), A (1st class), B, C, D and E. Prices are officially controlled.

Private accommodation is available on all the islands; in the larger towns it is best to enquire at the offices of the EOT (Greek Tourist Office) or the Tourist Police. In villages the landlord of the kafeníon will always help.

Holiday homes and flats may be rented through local travel agents.

Kiosks

Greek kiosks are amazing establishments. Every village has at least one; in the towns a kiosk stands on every square and at almost every crossroads. Almost everything essential for daily needs can be bought at a kiosk: newspapers, writing paper, ballpoint pens, cigarettes, souvenirs, sweets, razor blades, batteries, soap, combs, shampoo, matches, chewing gum and even a single-portion carton of instant coffee — the list seems to be quite inexhaustible. Kiosks are usually open until quite late at night.

Naturist facilities

Since September 1983 nudism has been permitted in enclosed areas which, with the consent of the community, are owned or leased to the enterprise concerned. Anywhere else nudism continues to be forbidden and is a punishable offence. Bare bosoms, on the other hand, are seen everywhere and are no longer of interest to the police — at least not in their official capacity!

Newspapers and magazines

British newspapers and some magazines are on sale in Corfu town and, during the summer months, in the other Ionian islands.

Opening times

Archaeological sites: see entry

Banks: see entry

Chemists: see entry

Museums: All museums are closed on Tuesdays and on January 1st, March 25th, Good Friday morning, Easter Day and Christmas Day.

Post offices: see entry

Shops: During the season shops are open on Monday, Wednesday and Saturday from 8.30 a.m.–2.30 p.m.; Tuesday, Thursday and Friday 8.30 a.m.–1.30 p.m. and 5–8 p.m.; in winter the hours vary.

Photography

A filter and a lens hood are essential because of the strength of the sun's rays.

The use of a hand-held camera is permitted on archaeological sites and, on payment of a fee, in museums (even with flash). A camera mounted on a tripod, however, may only be used if special permission has been obtained from Athens.

Post

Postal and telephone services in Greece are two separate concerns. Holidaymakers will not need to use post offices very often, as postage stamps can be purchased from most hotel reception desks, kiosks and shops. Any mail which is to be collected may be delivered to the post office in the appropriate town. It should be clearly marked with the words 'Post restan'.

Public Holidays

New Year's Day (January 1st); Epiphany (January 6th); Independence Day (March 25th); Okhi ('No') Day (October 28th — the day on which the Greeks rejected the Italian ultimatum in 1940); Christmas (December 25th and 26th).

In addition there are a number of other religious festivals (see page 15).

Radio and Television

There are two television channels and four radio stations in Greece. Many TV programmes are foreign productions with Greek sub-titles. News in English is transmitted early every morning on the first radio programme of the EPT 1 station.

Underwater fishing

Provided breathing apparatus is not used, anyone over the age of 18 may fish underwater, except around harbours and in areas where people swim. Fish weighing less than 150 grammes may not be harpooned.

Telephone

The telecommunications organisation *(OTE)* is responsible for telephones and telegrams. OTE offices are located in all the larger towns and many are open 24 hours a day. It is somewhat complicated to make a phone call from a telephone box (only the orange-coloured ones are suitable for trunk calls) but it is less expensive than from hotels and kiosks.

Time

Greece observes Eastern European Time which is two hours ahead of Greenwich Mean Time. From April to September clocks are advanced one hour.

Tipping

Tips are of course expected, as they are anywhere else in the world, and they certainly make life easier for the visitor. In the case of package tours it should not be assumed that tips are included in the cost. Good service and courtesy should be rewarded with a tip over and above the basic price; 10% of the bill is customary. As a rule waiters and domestic servants are poorly paid in Greece and they have to keep their families all the year round on what they earn from their seasonal jobs. If you eat out in an ordinary taverna do not, under any circumstances, forget the *mikrós*, the young boy who brings the drinks and cutlery; the tip is probably his only payment. Experienced travellers always give tips in hotels during their stay as well as when they leave.

Tourist Police

Tourist Police are found on most of the islands. They issue information and mediate in disputes between holidaymakers and hoteliers or landlords. They also deal with complaints, for example if a tourist thinks he is being overcharged.

Traffic regulations

As in most European countries, vehicles travel on the right and overtake on the left. Speed limits are 80 km p.h. on ordinary roads and 50 km p.h. in built-up areas. The horn may not be used in built-up areas and seat belts must be worn. A warning triangle must be carried. Drivers are prohibited from using a vehicle if they have drunk *any* alcohol.

Transport in the islands

Buses: A good bus service, run by the state (ΚΤΕΛ = *KTEL*), operates on all the islands. There is a bus station on every island where information may be obtained and tickets bought in advance.

Car hire, etc: Cars may be hired in all the Ionian islands, apart from Paxos and Ithaca, but the cost is high. Mopeds and motor scooters, sometimes even motorcycles, may be hired everywhere but are quite often in poor condition. More than half of all the foreign patients in Greek hospitals have had moped or scooter accidents!

Island hopping: With more than 200 inhabited islands, Greece is the ideal target for the enthusiastic 'island collector'. Hopping from island to island — not to be taken too literally of course — has only been possible up to now in the Aegean. Owing to the few inter-island connections, it is far more difficult to travel from one Ionian island to another by boat. Services from the islands operate principally to the mainland of Greece, and even the airports do not help the island-hopper very much, as most flights are only to or from Athens. The following is the only route which will take you to all the islands between Corfu and Zákinthos without your having to cross over to the mainland. This is the 'Island Hopping Route' with the name of the respective port on each island given in brackets: Corfu (Corfu town or Kávos) — Paxos (Gáios) – Ithaca (Vathí) – Lefkás (Nídri) – Cefalonia (arr. Fiskárdi, dep. Póros) – Killíni in the Peloponnese – Zákinthos (Zákinthos town).

Tickets and information: Tickets for individual stretches must always be purchased on the island which the passenger is leaving. You cannot buy a ticket for the whole journey, or return tickets. When several ships sail on one stretch of the route, the tickets are normally sold by different travel agents. Quite often each line has its own agent who is solely responsible for that particular line; when asked, the agent will often only give a quotation for his own connections and not for those of any rival company. This is why it is often better to obtain information from more than one bureau. The Greek Tourist Office (EOT) in Corfu will advise about the lines relevant to that island. Information can also be obtained from the Port Police on each of the islands and it is possible to phone them from any of the other islands.

Only small excursion boats operate the route from Lefkás to Ithaca and Cefalonia; they do not carry vehicles and sail only during the summer months. The services between the other islands are greatly reduced in winter.

Taxis : Travelling by taxi is cheaper than it is in Great Britain. There are two types of taxi: the genuine taxi (ΤΑΞΙ = *taksí*) which is equipped with a meter, and the *agoréon* (ΑΓΟΡΑΙΟΝ) which operates only in rural areas and does not have a meter. The fare charged for travelling a specified distance in an agoréon is fixed by the authorities and appears on a price-list which must be displayed in each vehicle. There is a taxi-rank with a telephone in most towns and resorts, from which taxis can be called or ordered in advance. For longer tours the price must be independently agreed with the driver.

Walking

Those who wish to use footpaths in Greece should note that there are no maps, signposts or printed guides for walkers. Footpaths, mule tracks and little-used dusty roads can however be found everywhere in the countryside. Three tips for walkers: if you have to ask a Greek the way, always add the word 'monopáthi' (footpath), otherwise you will be directed to a tarred road; mule tracks, which can be very stony, often lead through thorny undergrowth, and as poisonous snakes do occasionally appear, you are well advised to wear long trousers and stout footwear; a sun-hat is advisable.

Youth Hostels

Corfu is the only place in the Ionian islands with a youth hostel. This is restricted to members of the Youth Hostels Association.

Important Addresses

British Consulate
Leofóros Alexándras 11
Corfu Town; tel. (0661) 3 00 55, in emergency 3 92 11.

Offices of the Greek National Tourist Organisation (Ellinikós Organismós Tourismoú-EOT):

In UK
196-197 Regent Street
London W1R 8DL; tel. (01) 734 5997.

In Corfu
Governor's House
Corfu Town; tel. (0661) 3 03 60.

Information can also be obtained from the Tourist Police.

Idyllic Ionian scenery

Useful words and phrases

Although English is understood in many of the Ionian islands, the visitor will undoubtedly find a few words and phrases of Greek very useful. There is no standard system of transliteration from Greek into Roman script. In the examples given below an approximate pronunciation only is given. In modern Greek the stress on a word of more than one syllable is always shown by an accent.

The Greek alphabet

Α	α	Alpha	Ι	ι	Iota	Ρ	ρ	Rho
Β	β	Beta	Κ	κ	Kappa	Σ	σ	Sigma
Γ	γ	Gamma	Λ	λ	Lambda	Τ	τ	Tau
Δ	δ	Delta	Μ	μ	Mu	Υ	υ	Upsilon
Ε	ε	Epsilon	Ν	ν	Nu	Φ	φ	Phi
Ζ	ζ	Zeta	Ξ	ξ	Xi	Χ	χ	Chi
Η	η	Eta	Ο	ο	Omicron	Ψ	ψ	Psi
Θ	θ	Theta	Π	π	Pi	Ω	ω	Omega

In the pronunciation guide below the following should be noted:
dh = th in *this*; th = th in *thick*; kh = approximately the sound of ch in the Scottish word *loch*. Greek uses a semi-colon for a question mark.

please	parakaló	railway station	stathmós
thank you	efkharistó	exchange office	saráfiko
yes/no	ne *or* málista/ókhie	police station	astinomíkotmima
excuse me	mesinkhoríte	public telephone	tiléfono
do you speak English?	omelíte angliká?	information office	grafíopliroforíon
I do not understand	dhem katalaméno	doctor	yatrós
good morning/ afternoon	kaliméra	chemist	farmakío
		toilet	tooaléta
good evening	kalispéra	ladies	yinekón
good night	kaliníkhta	gentlemen	andhrón
good-bye	adío	engaged	katiliménos
how much?	póso káni?	free	eléftheros
a single room	dhomátio mé éna kreváti	entrance	isodhós
a double room	dhomátio mé dhio krevátia	exit	eksodhós
with bath	mé bánio / lutró	today / tomorrow	símera / ávrio
I should like	thaíthela	Sunday / Monday	kiriakí / dheftéra
the bill, please	to logariasmós parakaló	Tuesday / Wednesday	tríti / tetárti
everything included	óla simberilamvano- ménoo	Thursday / Friday	pémpti / paraskeví
		Saturday / holiday	sávato / skholí
open / shut	aniktós / klistós		
where is ... street?	pu iné to i odhós?	0 midhén	8 okhtó
... square?	i platía?	1 énas / éna	9 ennéa
how far?	póso makhriá?	2 dhío	10 dhéka
left	aristerá	3 tría	11 éndheka
right	dheksiá	4 téssera	12 dódheka
straight on	katefthían	5 pénde	20 íkosi
post office	takhidhromío	6 éksi	50 penínda
bank	trápesa	7 eftá	100 ekató

The meanings of names

On street signs and maps, in the names of places, monasteries, churches, natural features, etc., the same words occur again and again. It is helpful for the visitor to know what these words signify and so a selection will be found below together with their meanings in English.

Ágia	ΑΓΙΑ	saint (female)
Ágii	ΑΓΙΟΙ	saints
Ágios	ΑΓΙΟΣ	saint (male)
Akrotíri	ΑΚΡΩΤΗΡΙ	cape
Chóra	ΧΩΡΑ	island capital
Chorió	ΧΩΡΙΟ	village
Fáros	ΦΑΡΟΣ	lighthouse
Froúrio	ΦΡΟΥΡΙΟ	fortress/castle
Kástro	ΚΑΣΤΡΟ	fortress/castle
Kólpos	ΚΟΛΠΟΣ	bay
Leofóros	ΛΕΩΦΟΡΟΣ	boulevard/avenue
Limáni	ΛΙΜΑΝΙ	harbour
Límni	ΛΙΜΝΙ	lake/pond
Livádi	ΛΙΒΑΔΙ	meadow/pasture
Monastíri/Moni	ΜΟΝΑΣΤΗΡΙ/ΜΟΝΙ	monastery
Nisí/Nísos	ΝΗΣΙ/ΝΗΣΟΣ	island
Odós	ΟΔΟΣ	road/street
Órmos	ΟΡΜΟΣ	bay/anchorage
Óros	ΟΡΟΣ	mountain
Panagía	ΠΑΝΑΓΙΑ	Virgin Mary
Pantokrátor	ΠΑΝΤΟΚΡΑΤΩΡ	Ruler of the world (Christ)
Paralía	ΠΑΡΑΛΙΑ	beach/shore
Pélagos	ΠΕΛΑΓΟΣ	sea
Platía	ΠΛΑΤΕΙΑ	square
Pólis	ΠΟΛΙΣ	town
Potámi/Potamós	ΠΟΤΑΜΙ/ΠΟΤΑΜΟΣ	river/stream
Spíleo	ΣΠΗΛΑΙΟ	cave
Stavrós	ΣΤΑΥΡΟΣ	cross/crossing
Vathí	ΒΑΘΗ	depth/background
Áno/Epáno	ΑΝΩ/ΕΠΑΝΩ	upper/over
Archéa	ΑΡΧΑΙΑ	ancient
Káto	ΚΑΤΩ	under/lower
Méga/Megaló	ΜΕΓΑ/ΜΕΓΑΛΟ	great
Paleó	ΠΑΛΑΙΟ	old

INDEX

Original German text: Klaus Bötig. English translation: Angela Saunders. Cartography: Gert Oberländer. Series Editor – English edition: Alec Court.

Illustrations: Alan Boardman (pages 3, 14, 42); D. F. Goodrick (front cover and pages 38, 84, 85); Dick Elsden (pages 10, 17, 54, 59); Mary Pearce (pages 51, 57); Travel Trade Photography (pages 1, 20, 27, 30, 32, 34, 49, 69, 73, 75, 77, 79, 81); Caroline Jarrold (pages 53, 58, 60)

The publishers have made every endeavour to ensure the accuracy of this publication but can accept no responsibility for any errors or omissions. They would, however, appreciate notification of any inaccuracies to correct future editions.

Printed in Italy

ISBN 0-7117-0473-2